PRAISE FOR THE PU

In a time of increasing biblical illiteracy and con~~~~~~~~~~~~~~~~~~~ p.~~~~~~~ culture, Rice Broocks and Steve Murrell are calling Christians to a higher standard. If every Christian were to go through *The Purple Book* and prayerfully study it, I truly believe we would see Christians rising up and living the gospel with both clarity and power. I highly recommend this book for both individual and group study.

SEAN McDOWELL, Ph.D., Professor at Biola University, popular speaker, and author of more than fifteen books, including *A New Kind of Apologist*

I have done *The Purple Book* and know firsthand what an important discipleship tool it is. It gave me greater clarity on the importance of a strong biblical foundation and how to communicate that to others. It has been a joy to work in ministry with Rice and Steve and to witness its impact on lives around the world.

STORMIE OMARTIAN, Bestselling author of *The Power of a Praying* series, with more than thirty-two million books sold worldwide

The Purple Book helps ground believers in the foundational truths of the Christian faith. It's an effective tool that inspires you to engage with the life-changing power of Scripture.

DR. CRAIG KEENER, Professor at Ashbury Theological Seminary and author of the *NIV Bible Background Commentary*

The Purple Book is a compelling, comprehensive manual full of important information and biblical lessons that will help build a strong foundation in Christ. It is written by a dynamic duo of spiritual fathers who have raised a multitude of disciples who are now impacting almost every nation of the world. A must-read guide for anyone committed to building strong disciples.

BISHOP EFRAIM M. TENDERO, Secretary General / CEO of the World Evangelical Alliance

The Purple Book was a godsend to our church at a pivotal time—we needed a simple biblical resource to give to every person in our congregation to help shape the culture of discipleship. We have used thousands of these little books, and I tell pastors that it's the best resource ever for all people to use.

DR. FRANK DAMAZIO, Author and Pastor, Portland, Oregon

No aid, which has as its goal to establish biblical foundations in a person (or church's life), exceeds the simplicity or effectiveness of *The Purple Book*. Seldom a week passes when I have failed to help somebody better endure the storms of life by employing this study. It is the best and most often used tool in my ministry toolbox.

BRETT FULLER, Pastor of Grace Covenant Church, Chantilly, Virginia, and North American Director of Every Nation Churches

A foundational book on Christian doctrines, coming from reflective practitioners of movement discipleship. Tried, tested, and proven by Christians from all walks of life. *The Purple Book* is a Bible study guide on biblical faith; one that is faithful to Christian orthodoxy while emphasizing the presence and power of the Holy Spirit in the Christian life. Useful, handy, and recommended for every Christ follower!

TIM D. GENER, Ph.D., President and Professor of Theology at Asian Theological Seminary

THE
PURPLE
BOOK

updated edition

BIBLICAL FOUNDATIONS
FOR BUILDING STRONG DISCIPLES

RICE BROOCKS
AND STEVE MURRELL

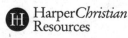 Harper*Christian*
Resources

CONTENTS

FOREWORD

Let's be honest: it's obvious we have a discipleship deficit in the church today. It's not true everywhere in the world, but it's true in the Western church. Christians everywhere are talking about discipleship and the necessity of a more robust approach to growing people in the knowledge and character of Jesus Christ. And it's in reaction to what leaders are seeing and perceiving in the general culture. In the West, we have a problem. Many of us are acknowledging it, and we have to fix it.

There are a lot of reasons for this discipleship deficit. Sometimes, it has to do with the shallowness of our theology. For others, it's individual laziness. And we can probably acknowledge at many junctures we are limited in discipleship because of a lack of systems that do not produce a comprehensive disciple-making journey. There is a deficit. So the question becomes: *what do we have to value to change the discipleship deficit?*

First, we have to start with an **individual's heart**. We have to have clear and simple discipleship processes that are constantly drawing us closer to Jesus so that we may know him and be changed by him. There is no substitute for the difficult but necessary internal character work that comes from being in proximity to Jesus and his Word, being changed by his Spirit, and being personally obedient to his Father's commandments.

Second, we have to focus on **multiplication**. We already know what happens when disciple-making becomes a multiplicative practice in an organization. Stories abound of people who have cracked the simplicity and multiplication code, seeing many come to Jesus and follow him rapidly. We have to find ways to disciple others and keep it simple enough to multiply quickly and easily.

Third, we have to create a **culture of discipleship**. This means that instead of being passive spectators, we become active participants in the mission of God. As leaders, we must participate in the discipleship process, model it to others, and shape an atmosphere of expectation for disciple-making. This won't just make us more knowledgeable, but also more godly by showing the love of Christ, sharing the hope of Christ, and serving others like Christ.

Someone once said, "No matter how beautiful the strategy, you should occasionally look at the results." However beautiful the disciple-making strategy, we have to look at the quality and quantity of disciples being made. In the West, we have a church culture that is anemic when it should be robust, lazy when it should be active, and obese with content and no activity when it should be lean with good content *and* activity. I want us to be a different kind of people: transformed by the power of the gospel and made into missional disciples for Jesus.

We have to find and rediscover a deep passion for discipleship. At LifeWay Research, we did a discipleship study called the "Transformational Discipleship Assessment," in which we studied more than 4,000 Protestant churchgoers and asked them about spiritual formation. Over the past few years, we've learned that:

- 54 percent of American Protestant churchgoers say they set aside time daily to a few times a week for private worship, praise, or thanksgiving to God (prayer not included).
- 42 percent of American Protestant churchgoers intentionally spend time with other believers in order to help them grow in their faith.
- 41 percent of American Protestant churchgoers do not attend small classes or groups from their churches.
- 25 percent of American Protestant churchgoers say they have shared their faith once or twice; 14 percent have shared three or more times over the last six months.
- 19 percent of American Protestant churchgoers read the Bible every day.

We have a long way to go. And to get there, we need a culture shift. Creating a culture of discipleship means reversing the discipleship deficit currently in the church. We have to recognize we are fighting a winnable, but uphill, battle.

The next question we have to ask is: *how are we going to actually change the discipleship deficit?* We have to have a clear pathway on the journey of disciple-making and acknowledge along the way that there are some things that deeply matter. I'm convinced (and have preached or shared on this subject) that we are missing the mark on discipleship if we don't see maturity as a goal for a disciple. God wants the people in our churches to be on a path toward spiritual maturity, and he involves us in our own growth as well as the church's growth.

Paul writes of this path in his letter to the Colossians:

> For this reason also, since the day we heard this, we haven't stopped praying for you. We are asking that you may be filled with the knowledge of his will in all wisdom and spiritual understanding, so that you may walk worthy of the Lord, fully pleasing to Him, bearing fruit in every good work and growing in the knowledge of God (Colossians 1:9–10 HCSB).

There are three ways we can change discipleship for the better:

First, **knowing**. Being "filled with the knowledge of God's will" and "growing in the knowledge of God" is a vital part of becoming a disciple of Jesus. We can instruct people to be like Jesus, but if they don't *know* him it is impossible to be *like* him. A key to knowing Jesus is saturating ourselves in God's Word. Psalm 119 says, "Your word is a lamp for my feet and a light on my path" (Psalm 119:105 HCSB). As we read the Scriptures, they shine the light brighter in our lives, and we are able to see and stay on the path of spiritual maturity.

Second, **being**. Being "worthy of the Lord" extends beyond our knowledge to who we are in Christ to how we rest in Christ and his work on the cross, for our sins, and in our place. As we follow Jesus in discipleship and maturity, there is a transfer of who he is into who we are. It is like a blood transfusion, changing our being into his in every area of life. Paul says, "Do not be conformed to this age, but be transformed by the renewing of your mind" (Romans 12:2 HCSB). We walk worthy of the Lord when we take on his traits and our actions flow out of who we are becoming as a result of our proximity to him.

Third, **doing**. "Bearing fruit" is another way we change discipleship from the classroom to the front lines. Knowing who we are in Christ (knowledge), then being who we are in Christ (walking worthy), leads us to doing the work of Christ (bearing fruit). We are designed to produce fruit. In Ephesians 2, Paul gives us God's plan for what that looks like: "For we are His creation, created in Christ Jesus for good works, which God prepared ahead of time so that we should walk in them" (Ephesians 2:10 HCSB). God has prepared for us practical outworking of our faith as followers of Jesus, and we should boldly live our lives to love and serve others out of Jesus and his Spirit's empowerment within us.

For a long time now, I've found that if I want to do something, I need to find someone who is doing it right and learn from them. So is the case for Rice Broocks and Steve Murrell with their newly updated version of *The Purple Book*. *The Purple Book* is the type of resource that has begun to shape their movement with robust disciple-makers. More than a million copies are now in print, and both my wife and I have worked through *The Purple Book* in my own home.

We all need a simple and effective disciple-making tool that creates a culture, gives a pathway for multiplication, and focuses on the individual's heart first. We can grow in knowledge, become more like Jesus, and bear much fruit by putting into practice the many helpful tools that Rice and Steve provide.

I hope you will be as encouraged and challenged by this book as I was!

Ed Stetzer
Billy Graham Distinguished Chair of Church, Mission, and Evangelism at Wheaton College

PREFACE

Anyone who wants God's best for their life must begin by building a strong foundation. Jesus said as much when he declared, "As for everyone who comes to me and hears my words and puts them into practice, I will show you what they are like. They are like a man building a house, who dug down deep and laid the foundation on rock. When a flood came, the torrent struck that house but could not shake it, because it was well built" (Luke 6:47–48). He then contrasted this wise man with one who was foolish, who heard but failed to act and found himself living in a house built on sand.

Both had their works tested by the storms of life—storms that come even more often in today's uncertain world. And in this real-life game of *Survivor*, only one person was left standing. The large number of damaged and/or collapsed lives in today's church is testimony to the pressing need to once again build strong foundations.

Several years ago, I took a team of students to the island of Guam for an evangelistic outreach. Checking into my hotel, I was given what would later prove to be a prophetic sign. "Sir," the clerk said as she handed me my key, "your room is 911." Everyone joked about how I would be getting all the emergency calls.

Two days later, one of the century's worst earthquakes—8.2 on the Richter scale—jolted the island. Even more incredible, it lasted for sixty bone-chilling seconds. Inside room 911, the world seemed to explode. The television hurtled to the floor. Slammed from its perch, the sliding glass door shattered into a million pieces.

We ran for the fire escape only to find the route blocked. With nowhere else to go, we stood on the balcony, riding out the most terrifying minute of our lives. With each tremor came a growing certainty that the building would soon collapse. We were about to die!

Suddenly, just as it felt like the hotel would rip in half, all motion ceased. We found a way out and made our way to the street, singing the praises of our God. Never had I found a more humble audience and had an easier time telling strangers about the Lord!

The next day, we toured the island to assess the damage. One of the images that stood out was a brand-new hotel now on the verge of collapse. Two of its floors had disintegrated, and the rest of the structure tilted like the Leaning Tower of Pisa. Before the quake, it appeared perfectly sound. But the storm of this earthquake revealed what was really there beneath the surface. Because the foundations were faulty, the entire building had to be torn down.

Thankfully, the engineers who designed our hotel did not make the same mistakes. Though it cost them time and money, they took into account the fact that they were building in an earthquake zone, designing and building the foundations accordingly.

There is an important lesson in all of this. We, too, live along a "fault line." The tectonic plates of sin are pushing hard against us. From the Middle East to our middle schools—everywhere—we see massive upheaval. If we are going to build lives that will stand, not just any foundation will do.

> For no one can lay any foundation other than the one already laid, which is Jesus Christ (1 Corinthians 3:11).

We must dig down deep and tear out everything that is hostile to Christ. We must hear his words—particularly those that deal with the very foundations of faith—and obey.

The book you hold in your hands will teach you these great foundational truths. It will help bring alive the words that the apostle Paul shared with a young man who was also seeking to build his life upon the rock:

> All Scripture is God-breathed and is useful for teaching, rebuking, correcting and training in righteousness, so that the servant of God may be thoroughly equipped for every good work (2 Timothy 3:16–17).

Most of us like the teaching part. But far fewer of us are thrilled about being rebuked or corrected. The fact is, however, that it is the latter that separates the winners from the losers. There is no way to be equipped for a good work—or a good life—without God's Word doing a deep work in us. And there is no way to be a disciple without being disciplined. Who has ever heard of a successful athlete, soldier, musician, or scientist who has not subjected themselves to a strict regimen of training and discipline? And so it must be for the children of light.

We are living in one of the greatest times in church history. Technology has drawn the world so tightly together that we can realistically hope to reach every nation and tribe and language with the Gospel. But with this great opportunity comes an even greater responsibility. It is vital that the faith we preach is the one that we live out—in all its powerful, life-and-nation-transforming glory.

The early church turned their world upside down. They reached multitudes without jets, computers, the Internet—not even a sound system! What spoke the loudest was their lives. People saw the transforming power of Christ in the men and women who left everything to follow him. The fault lines that ran through the Roman Empire, and the many earthquakes (both literal and spiritual) that followed, only tested their foundations and helped them stand when everything else around them came crashing down.

Let us pray for a new generation to come forth, pledging their all, doing their part to help turn the world back to righteousness.

Rice Broocks
Cofounder, Every Nation Churches & Ministries

CHAPTER ONE

SIN & SALVATION

In the beginning God created the heavens and the earth . . .

GENESIS 1:1

Through him all things were made; without him nothing was made that has been made . . .

JOHN 1:3

All things have been created through him and for him.

COLOSSIANS 1:16

The earth, humanity—all that we see around us—had a beginning.

God declared each phase of creation "good"—until he created the first man, Adam, and said that it was "not good" for him to be alone.

So God created Eve, the first woman, and gave the original couple everything to enjoy. They were only forbidden to eat the fruit of one tree: the "tree of the knowledge of good and evil."

The fatal decision that followed and its tragic results have affected all of human history. Humanity would pass down this fatal flaw, this inner corruption, from generation to generation. The power of evil and darkness would have prevailed—except for God's intervention. His plan of salvation, of deliverance from evil's power, began to unfold in that very Garden of Eden. This is the primary story of the entire Bible.

LESSON 1

THE ORIGINAL STORY

1. What was creation like in the beginning (Genesis 1)?

    verse 10 _____
    verse 12 _____
    verse 18 _____
    verse 21 _____
    verse 25 _____

2. How many commands did God give Adam and Eve (Genesis 2:17)?

    _____

3. What was God's command to the first human beings (Genesis 2:16–17)?

    _____
    _____

Read Genesis 3:1–13 to find out what happened next.

4. How did Adam and Eve respond to God's command (Genesis 3:6–7)?

    _____
    _____
    _____

5. In light of this, do you think that you would have responded any differently?

_____

Think about what God attempted to shield Adam and Eve from: the knowledge of evil. What loving parents today don't do everything possible to protect their children from dangerous material—on television, on the Internet or anywhere else?

6. Who tempted Eve (Genesis 3:1)?

_____

Adam and Eve ate the forbidden fruit—in essence saying to God, "We don't need you or your rules." They disobeyed God. They *sinned*.

7. How did Adam and Eve react after their eyes were opened and they realized they were naked (Genesis 3)?

verse 7 _____

verse 8 _____

verse 10 _____

8. Why do you think they reacted this way?

_____

_____

9. How did God respond to Adam and Eve's sin (Genesis 3:8-9)?

_____

_____

Notice the two very different responses to humanity's sin:

- Humanity covered up and hid from God.
- God sought humanity.

Things have not changed much since the beginning. After thousands of years and billions of people, human beings still hide from God—and God still seeks. This is the starting point for understanding salvation.

Application & Reflection
What did you learn from this lesson? How will you apply it to your life?

_____

_____

_____

_____

_____

LESSON 2

THE RESULTS OF SIN
The act of disobeying God is called *sin*. One definition of sin is to "miss the mark," as when you fail to hit the target in a sporting event.

Obviously, the Bible's understanding of sin is much more serious than that. In fact, Scripture has a couple different ways of expressing this idea. Sin is sometimes described as a *trespass*, which is something that involves crossing forbidden lines or boundaries that God sets up for our protection.

The concept of *iniquity* speaks of sin's most troubling and destructive result: to twist and pervert our inner nature. This is gravely serious because the Bible says God's nature is *holy*—that is, completely free from evil or defect, absolutely pure in love and goodness.

1. What state does the Bible describe us as being in (Ephesians 2:1)?

_____

2. Why ultimately is our sin so serious to God (Leviticus 11:44)?

_____

3. What does iniquity do to our relationship with God (Isaiah 59:1-2)?

_____

4. How would you describe sinful humanity's desperate condition (Romans 3:9-20, 23)?

_____

5. What impact has sin had on the human heart (Jeremiah 17:9)?

_____

6. What are the "wages of sin" (Romans 6:23)?

_____

7. What does the Bible say happens after we die (Hebrews 9:27)?

_____

8. How does the Bible describe eternal judgment?

Matthew 25:41 _____

1 Thessalonians 1:9–10 _____

Revelation 21:8 _____

9. What does Paul, the writer of Romans, call himself (Romans 7:24)?

_____

In Romans 7, Paul describes his own state and cries out on behalf of all humanity with the most important question ever asked: "Who will rescue me from this body that is subject to death?" (verse 24). Humanity's deepest need is for salvation—not just from the evil in the world, but also from the evil in our own hearts.

Application & Reflection

Obviously, God takes sin very seriously. What about you? What do you think you deserve for your sin?

_____

_____

_____

_____

LESSON 3

GOD'S SOLUTION FOR SIN: JESUS' DEATH AND RESURRECTION

The penalty for sin is death, both spiritual and physical. God's ultimate solution for sin was foreshadowed in the original story in the Garden of Eden. After Adam and Eve sinned, they tried to hide themselves with their own covering—and humanity has been trying to hide from God ever since. God, however, provided the real covering, and he did so by spilling the blood of an innocent animal.

The concept of sacrifice (the idea that someone has to pay the penalty for sin) is seen throughout the Bible. Sin was forgiven only as a result of shedding blood—a sacrifice offered in the place of sinful human beings. The sacrifice had to be one without defect.

1. What is necessary for the forgiveness of sins (Hebrews 9:22)?

   _____

2. How did God cover Adam and Eve's first sin (Genesis 3:21)?

   _____

3. What did God require for forgiveness to occur (Hebrews 9:22)?

   _____

4. Can the blood of animals ultimately take away our sin (Hebrews 10:4)?

_____

Read Isaiah 53.

5. Why would the promised Savior be "pierced" (Isaiah 53:5)?

_____

6. How does the prophet Isaiah say we will be healed (Isaiah 53:5)?

_____

7. How did John the Baptist, the last great prophet before Jesus, introduce Jesus publicly (John 1:29)?

_____

_____

8. What did the prophet Isaiah predict God would do (Isaiah 53:6)?

_____

9. What does Jesus' blood—his sacrificial death—do for us?

Romans 5:9 _____

Ephesians 1:7 _____

Ephesians 2:13 _____

1 John 1:7 _____

Revelation 1:5 _____

10. What did Jesus do for us on the cross?

1 Corinthians 15:3–4 _____

2 Corinthians 5:21 _____

Galatians 3:13–14 _____

1 Peter 2:24 _____

11. According to the Bible, what makes Jesus unique so he can do this for us?

    John 1:18 _____
    Colossians 1:15–20 _____
    Hebrews 4:15 _____

Jesus' blood—his sacrificial death—is God's solution for humanity's sin. He pays the penalty for our sin. He wants to wipe the slate clean—forgiveness. But Jesus didn't just stay in the grave. He rose from the dead.

12. What is the significance of Jesus' resurrection? What if there was no resurrection (1 Corinthians 15:14–19)?

    verse 14 _____
    verse 15 _____
    verse 16 _____
    verse 17 _____
    verse 18 _____
    verse 19 _____

What makes God's gift of grace so costly is that Jesus paid for it with his life. What makes it so powerful is that he came back from the dead—proving that he is the Son of God and showing that God accepted his sacrifice as payment for our sin.

> He was delivered over to death for our sins and was raised to life for our justification (Romans 4:25).

God's law demands that sin be punished by death. Year in and year out, innocent animals would die in the place of God's people, reminding them that sin is costly. However, God's plan was to send his ultimate sacrifice, Jesus Christ, as a "lamb" to be offered for the sins of the whole world. Even more amazing is the fact that the Bible calls

Jesus "Immanuel," which means "God with us." God became a man in Jesus Christ and died for the sins of his own creation.

Application & Reflection

What did you learn from this lesson? How will you apply it to your life?

_____

_____

_____

_____

_____

LESSON 4

RECEIVING GOD'S GIFT: A NEW HEART

As a result of receiving God's sacrifice through Jesus Christ as the payment for our sins, we not only experience forgiveness from the past but are also given a new heart and a new life as God's children.

1. What did God promise he would give his people (Ezekiel 36:26)?

_____

2. What does God do when he rescues us from our state of spiritual death (Ephesians 2:4-6)?

_____

3. What happens when we receive Jesus as our Lord and Savior (John 1:12-13)?

_____

4. What did Jesus say must happen before we can enter the kingdom of God (John 3:3-7)?

_____

5. What do the following passages tell you about being "born again" or "born of God"?

John 1:12–13 _____

1 Peter 1:23 _____

1 John 3:9 _____

1 John 4:7 _____

6. What does Paul say about those who are "in Christ" (2 Corinthians 5:17)?

_____

_____

7. What is the destiny of those who are "born of God" (1 John 5:4)?

_____

Application & Reflection

What would you do if someone could offer you a brand-new start in life? Have you received God's gift of new life?

_____

_____

_____

_____

LESSON 5

GRACE THROUGH FAITH

It is critical to understand that we cannot save ourselves. The foundation of our faith is Jesus' death and resurrection. That's what paid the penalty for our sins. As a result of God's work in Jesus, we are a new people with a new heart and a new Lord.

1. Is it possible to be saved *by* the good things we do—our "works"? How are we saved (Ephesians 2:8–9)?

   _____

   _____

   _____

2. Does God save us *because* of the good things we do? If not, why does he save us (Titus 3:4–5)?

   _____

   _____

3. What does God's grace teach the believer (Titus 2:11–12)?

   _____

   _____

4. Should we continue to sin because of God's forgiveness and grace (Romans 6:15)?

   _____

   _____

5. What are we created for as new Christians (Ephesians 2:10)?

   _____

   _____

6. What did Jesus say to those who believed in him (Matthew 16:24)?

   _____

   _____

As we have learned in this chapter, we are spiritually dead and cannot save ourselves. Regardless of who we are, we need a Savior. Jesus Christ is the only true Savior. By receiving Jesus as Savior and Lord, we can be delivered from the power of sin and its consequences. Our salvation is based on what Jesus did for us, not on our own efforts.

We must therefore . . .

> **Realize** that we are sinners without excuse (Romans 1:20) and that it is only through the death and resurrection of Jesus Christ that we can be saved.

> **Respond** by turning from sin, putting our faith in him, and then following him as Lord (Acts 3:19).

In the next two chapters, we will thoroughly examine what it means to now be followers of Jesus.

Application & Reflection
What did you learn from this lesson? How will you apply it to your life?

CHAPTER TWO

LORDSHIP & OBEDIENCE

*"For I command you today to love the LORD your God,
to walk in obedience to him, and to keep his commands,
decrees and laws; then you will live."*

MOSES, DEUTERONOMY 30:16

*"Why do you call me, 'Lord, Lord,' and do not do what I say?
As for everyone who comes to me and hears my words and puts
them into practice, I will show you what they are like. They are
like a man building a house, who dug down deep and laid the
foundation on rock. When a flood came, the torrent struck that
house but could not shake it, because it was well built."*

JESUS, LUKE 6:46-48

"If you love me, keep my commands."

JESUS, JOHN 14:15

To say that Jesus is Lord is to say that he is not only the Son of God
but also that he is God himself in the flesh. Realizing this shows the

greatness and grandeur of God's love—that he would become a man and die for us. This revelation changes our hearts and minds forever. Christ's lordship also means that his words are truly God's words—and must be trusted and obeyed.

To say that we must trust and obey Christ doesn't mean that salvation depends on us being perfect. Rather, following Jesus as Lord is the *attitude* of complete surrender and obedience to Jesus Christ.

LESSON 1

JESUS IS LORD

1. What did Peter (one of Jesus' disciples) proclaim about Christ (Acts 2:36)?

_____

Lord is another word for "master." *Messiah* means "anointed one" and is a special term for Jesus, indicating that he's the deliverer God had promised to send.

2. What did Paul write about Jesus (Philippians 2:6–11)?

verse 6 _____
verse 7 _____
verse 8 _____
verse 9 _____
verse 10 _____
verse 11 _____

3. What does Paul say we should do after we receive Jesus (Colossians 2:6)?

_____

_____

4. What did Jesus say was the result of not obeying him (Luke 6:46–49)?

5. According to Jesus, who will enter the kingdom of heaven (Matthew 7:21–23)?

Application & Reflection
What did you learn from this lesson? How will you apply it to your life?

LESSON 2

THE NARROW DOOR
The Bible teaches that we are saved by God's grace, not by our own good deeds. We cannot earn eternal life through good behavior. We must receive the gift of Jesus' work on the cross. However, when true salvation occurs, the evidence of our changed lives should be obvious.

Read Matthew 7:13–20 to find out what Jesus had to say about what it means to be his true follower.

1. What does Jesus say about entering the kingdom of God?

verses 13–14

2. How can we tell who is a real follower of Jesus and who is not?

verse 16 _____

3. According to Jesus, what is the destiny of those who bear bad fruit?

verse 19 _____

"Bad fruit" is a metaphor for a sinful lifestyle. Sin is lawlessness. It's breaking God's commands.

4. Centuries before Jesus was born, God gave his people the Law–summed up in the Ten Commandments. What are God's Ten Commandments (Exodus 20:1-17)?

verse 3 _____
verses 4–6 _____
verse 7 _____
verses 8–10 _____
verse 12 _____
verse 13 _____
verse 14 _____
verse 15 _____
verse 16 _____
verse 17 _____

5. What did Jesus say about those who disregard these laws (Matthew 5:17-19)?

_____
_____

The Bible declares that Jesus Christ is the source of our righteousness (our right standing with God). Yet God's laws have not been done away with. There is still such a thing as right and wrong. When we break these laws, it is still called "sin." The difference is that now, as Christians, we not only can be forgiven but also have a new ability to say no to sin.

6. How did Jesus say we could sum up all of God's law (Matthew 7:12)?

7. What is the difference between those who love Jesus and those who do not (John 14:15, 23–24)?

8. What does Paul say must not be in our lives as believers (Ephesians 5:3–5)?

9. What did Paul warn would happen to those who practice such things (Galatians 5:19–21)?

10. What is the reason that people live in sin and still think they are Christians (1 Corinthians 6:9–10)?

These warnings remind us that we are not just new people in theory, but that we are called to live in a new way. As humans, we certainly won't be perfect, but because of Christ, we are on a journey that will lead to greater and greater victories over the sins and weaknesses that previously dominated our lives. This process is called sanctification.

And that is what some of you were. But you were washed, you were sanctified, you were justified in the name of the Lord Jesus Christ and by the Spirit of our God (1 Corinthians 6:11).

Application & Reflection
What did you learn from this lesson? How will you apply it to your life?

_____

_____

_____

_____

LESSON 3

LORDSHIP AND RELATIONSHIPS

The Bible talks a lot about *fellowship*. Fellowship is more than hanging out with others; it's *sharing life* with them. It's opening our lives to other followers of Jesus and living in community with them. While God doesn't want us to abandon our relationships with unbelievers and isolate ourselves from the world, authentic fellowship is something that is experienced in its fullest with other believers.

1. According to the Bible, what kind of people should we avoid altogether (1 Corinthians 5:11)?

   _____

   _____

2. In one of his letters, Paul mentions a particularly disturbing case of immorality. What did Paul say the church should have done (1 Corinthians 5:1-2)?

   _____

   _____

3. What did Paul say about "fellowship" with unbelievers (2 Corinthians 6:14-16)?

   _____

   _____

4. What does God command (2 Corinthians 6:17)?

_____

5. What does he promise in return (2 Corinthians 6:18)?

_____

To "be separate" doesn't mean we should cut ourselves off from the rest of the world. After all, Jesus also tells us to be "salt and light" to the world (Matthew 5:13–16), and we can't be salt and light from a distance. Jesus himself was criticized for being a friend of sinners (Luke 15:1–2). But like Jesus, God wants us to have a transforming influence on the world around us—not the other way around.

6. How does John say we know we "have passed from death to life" (1 John 3:14)?

_____

_____

7. How many times did Jesus say we should forgive our brothers and sisters (Matthew 18:21–22)?

_____

_____

8. As we live in love and unity with one another, what did Jesus promise would be the world's response (John 17:23)?

_____

_____

9. What is a key to having this kind of unity (Philippians 2:3–4)?

_____

_____

The quality of our relationships with other believers is a crucial testimony to an unbelieving world. We should be able to forgive and love not just our friends, but also our enemies. We must realize that we are in a spiritual battle, and we must be trained and determined not to allow bitterness and unforgiveness to push us into darkness.

Application & Reflection

What do you think it means to be in the world but not of the world (John 17:15–18)?

_____

_____

_____

_____

_____

_____

LESSON 4

CAN YOU PASS THE TEST?

The book of 1 John describes how we can evaluate the real condition of our lives. *Deception* is a very powerful force. The devil is the master deceiver, and many have fallen under the influence of his deception. Many have prayed prayers, attended Bible studies, or even joined a church—but their lives have not been truly changed by Jesus.

This lesson underscores the Bible's teaching that as Christians saved by grace, we are expected to live in a new way—in relation to God and to each other.

1. What is the message that John proclaimed (1 John 1:5)?

_____

2. What does John say about those who claim to have fellowship with God and yet continue to walk in darkness (1 John 1:6)?

_____

_____

3. What does the Bible say about people who claim to be Christians but do not follow God's commands (1 John 2:3-4)?

_____

_____

4. What does God command?

1 John 3:11 _____

Matthew 22:34–40 _____

5. What does John say about those who claim to love God but hate their fellow believers (1 John 2:9-11)?

_____

_____

6. How can we know the difference between "children of God" and "children of the devil" (1 John 3:7-10)?

_____

_____

7. If we say we love God yet hate a brother or sister, what does the Bible say we are (1 John 4:20)?

_____

_____

This may seem hard to us, but if we embrace the truth, we will be changed. Jesus' death on the cross paid the price for our sin. His resurrection broke the power of sin and death. In light of the power of the cross and resurrection, why would we want to accept a gospel that does not transform our lives and liberate us from sin?

In the next chapter, we will examine the necessary response to the message of Jesus' lordship.

Application & Reflection
What did you learn from this lesson? How will you apply it to your life?

_____

_____

_____

_____

_____

CHAPTER THREE

REPENTANCE & BAPTISM

"Repent and be baptized, every one of you . . ."

PETER, ACTS 2:38

"Repent, then, and turn to God, so that your sins may be wiped out, that times of refreshing may come from the Lord."

PETER, ACTS 3:19

One of the most gripping stories in the Bible concerns a relationship crisis between a father and a son (Luke 15:11–24). Jesus told this story of a son who took his inheritance and went away and squandered it with "wild living." He ended up losing everything and living in despair. The Bible says the son eventually "came to his senses" and determined to get up and return to his father. This is a picture of what is meant by repentance—in essence, being truly sorry for our sins and desperate to restore our relationship with God, our heavenly Father.

LESSON 1

WHAT SHALL WE DO?

1. What did the prodigal son say to his father (Luke 15:21)?

2. What was the response of the father (Luke 15:22–24)?

3. What did Jesus say causes heaven to celebrate (Luke 15:7)?

Repentance produces a real change in our hearts and is the fruit of God's grace truly working in our lives. Read Acts 2:36–47.

4. Who did Peter declare Jesus Christ to be (Acts 2:36)?

5. What did the people say in response to Peter's preaching (Acts 2:37)?

6. What did Peter say they should do (Acts 2:38)?

7. What did Peter say they would receive if they would repent and be baptized (Acts 2:38)?

8. Who did this promise apply to (Acts 2:39)?

9. What else did Peter say (Acts 2:40)?

_____

_____

10. What happened to those who accepted the message (Acts 2:41)?

_____

_____

11. Once they were added to the local body of believers, what did they do (Acts 2:42–46)?

_____

_____

Peter preached the message of the cross—that Jesus is both Lord and Messiah. The result? The people were "cut to the heart." They responded by asking, "What shall we do?" The answer to their question was fourfold:

- Repent.
- Be baptized.
- Receive the gift of the Holy Spirit.
- Be added to the church (the community of believers).

In this chapter, we will study repentance and water baptism. The Holy Spirit and the church will be covered in separate chapters.

Application & Reflection

What did you learn from this lesson? How will you apply it to your life?

_____

_____

_____

_____

LESSON 2

REPENTANCE: TURNING FROM SIN

1. What message did Jesus preach (Mark 1:15)?

_____

2. What message should be preached in all nations (Luke 24:47)?

_____

3. What happens when we repent and turn to God (Acts 3:19)?

_____

4. What promise do we have from God when we repent of our sins (1 John 1:9)?

_____

_____

The word *repentance* often brings to mind scary images of people on a street corner with signs reading, "Repent, for the end is near!" Actually, the possibility of repentance offers great hope for us. It means to "turn around." Regardless of how bad things have gotten or how far away we may *feel* from God, when we repent (turn), we instantly find God's love and mercy waiting for us.

5. What did Jesus say would happen if we don't repent (Luke 13:2–5)?

_____

6. Who does God command to repent (Acts 17:30)?

_____

7. What did the apostle Paul say he was sent to do (Acts 26:18)?

_____

_____

8. What message did Paul say he preached (Acts 26:19–20)?

9. How did Paul tell his listeners they could demonstrate their repentance (Acts 26:20)?

10. What should we do about our sins (Proverbs 28:13)?

11. True repentance involves confession of sin, turning away from sin, and turning to God. What else is involved (Exodus 22:3)?

Restitution is defined as "a restoration of something to its rightful owner" and "a making good of . . . for some injury" (*Merriam-Webster's Collegiate Dictionary*, eleventh edition). Read Luke 19:1–10 for a story about repentance and restitution.

12. Zacchaeus was a corrupt tax collector. Yet the opportunity of a relationship with Jesus inspired him to repent and make restitution for his sins. How did he propose to make restitution (Luke 19:8)?

13. How did Jesus respond to Zacchaeus (Luke 19:9)?

14. What leads us toward repentance (Romans 2:4)?

15. Part of repentance is being sorry for our sins. What are the two types of sorrow, and what do they produce (2 Corinthians 7:10)?

_____

_____

16. Besides repentance, what else does godly sorrow produce (2 Corinthians 7:11)?

_____

According to the Bible, repentance involves conviction of sin, sorrow for sin, turning from sin, and a willingness to make restitution. However, repentance is still not complete without faith.

Application & Reflection
What did you learn from this lesson? How will you apply it to your life?

_____

_____

_____

LESSON 3

REPENTANCE: TURNING TO GOD
True conversion is like the two sides of a coin. One side is repentance; the other side is faith. We cannot turn from something without turning to something else. All of this is a gift of God (Ephesians 2:8).

1. What did Paul say we must turn to when we turn from darkness (Acts 26:18)?

_____

2. What was the result of the miraculous healing of a paralyzed man (Acts 9:35)?

_____

3. What was the evidence that the "Lord's hand" was with those who proclaimed Christ (Acts 11:21)?

_____

_____

Probably the most quoted Scripture of all is John 3:16:

> For God so loved the world that he gave his one and only Son, that whoever believes in him shall not perish but have eternal life.

Believing in Christ means more than merely saying the right words or accepting certain facts. It means that we put our trust completely in him. In essence, real faith implies that we reject all other alternatives and fix our attention on him.

4. Is simply saying we believe in God enough (James 2:19)?

_____

5. What does the Bible say about faith without any corresponding works (James 2:26)?

_____

6. What is the promise for those who truly believe (John 6:47)?

_____

7. Who does the Bible say overcomes the world (1 John 5:4–5)?

_____

The hope of every believer is that Christ's work in us is more powerful than our past or our current struggles and temptations. The picture of salvation the Bible paints is not just a glorious deliverance, but also God's Spirit empowering us to live new lives. The next important step in our journey is to follow Christ in baptism.

Application & Reflection
What did you learn from this lesson? How will you apply it to your life?

_____

_____

_____

_____

_____

LESSON 4

WATER BAPTISM

If you take a trip to Israel and tour the ancient land where Jesus lived and ministered, you'll discover that the world of the Bible included the concept of ritual bathing. Men and women would wash ceremonially to cleanse themselves from the dirt and defilement of the outside world. Jesus and his disciples came preaching and calling people to be baptized in water to symbolize the cleansing that takes place through their faith. In the Great Commission, Jesus would command his disciples, "Go and make disciples of all nations, baptizing them in the name of the Father and of the Son and of the Holy Spirit" (Matthew 28:19).

1. What happened to those who accepted Peter's message (Acts 2:41)?

_____

2. What did the men and women who believed Philip's message do (Acts 8:12)?

_____

3. After hearing the good news about Jesus, what did the Ethiopian eunuch want to do (Acts 8:35–36)?

_____

4. Jesus told his disciples to go and make disciples of all nations. What did he say to do with those disciples (Matthew 28:19-20)?

verse 19 _____

verse 20 _____

The New Testament uses four different illustrations to help us understand the significance of water baptism:

- Burial and resurrection (Romans 6:4–5)
- The Israelites crossing the Red Sea when they escaped from Egypt (1 Corinthians 10:1–2)
- Circumcision (Colossians 2:11–12)
- The flood (1 Peter 3:20–21)

5. Paul compares Christian baptism to a burial. In order to be buried, a person must first die. What must we die to before we can be baptized (Romans 6:1-4)?

_____

_____

6. The Israelites' passing through the Red Sea is a picture of baptism for us. Why were the Israelites fleeing from the Egyptians (Exodus 2:23; 3:7, 9)?

_____

_____

7. What happened to the Egyptians (Exodus 14:22-28)?

_____

_____

In the same way the Israelites were slaves to the Egyptians, we were all slaves to sin. The Israelites were freed from their bondage by passing through the Red Sea. Baptism pictures the freedom from sin that Jesus purchased for us on the cross.

8. Paul says baptism is like a circumcision not done by human hands, but a circumcision done by Christ. What is put off during this spiritual circumcision (Colossians 2:11–12)?

9. What did Peter say the flood water symbolized (1 Peter 3:21)?

10. What is baptism a pledge of (1 Peter 3:21)?

Peter teaches that it is not the "removal of dirt from the body" that saves us. In other words, it is neither the *act* of baptism nor the *water* of baptism. Rather, it is "the resurrection of Jesus Christ" that saves us. Once again we see the Scriptures teaching that we are saved by what Jesus did (his death and resurrection), not by what we do (water baptism). Peter goes on to say that baptism is the pledge of a clear conscience.

Each of the Bible's pictures of baptism shows the old life being put away and a new life emerging. In baptism we publicly display what Jesus did through his death and resurrection. We also show that we have identified with this. By obeying his command to be baptized, we identify with the power of the cross and resurrection to deliver us completely from the power and authority of sin. *"And now what are you waiting for? Get up, be baptized and wash your sins away, calling on his name"* (Acts 22:16).

Application & Reflection
What did you learn from this lesson? How will you apply it to your life?

THE HOLY SPIRIT & SPIRITUAL GIFTS

"I baptize you with water for repentance. But after me comes one who is more powerful than I . . . . He will baptize you with the Holy Spirit and fire."

JOHN THE BAPTIST, MATTHEW 3:11

"But the Advocate, the Holy Spirit, whom the Father will send in my name, will teach you all things and will remind you of everything I have said to you."

JESUS, JOHN 14:26

"Repent and be baptized, every one of you, in the name of Jesus Christ for the forgiveness of your sins. And you will receive the gift of the Holy Spirit."

PETER, ACTS 2:38

Before Jesus ascended to heaven, he told his disciples to go back to Jerusalem and wait. They were about to receive an amazing gift: the baptism of the Holy Spirit.

A few days later, during the Jewish festival of Pentecost, the Spirit came . . . and he didn't come quietly. He arrived in wind and fire. Suddenly the believers began speaking in other tongues. Jews from all over the Roman Empire had gathered in Jerusalem for the festival—and each of them heard the believers speak to them in their own language!

Then Peter got up to speak. He reminded the crowd that hundreds of years earlier, the prophet Joel had predicted that God's Spirit would come. Peter proclaimed Jesus' death and resurrection. The crowd, cut to the heart, responded, "What shall we do?"

Peter said the proper response would be to repent, be baptized, and receive the gift of the Holy Spirit. In other words, it is impossible to live the Christian life apart from the power and presence of the Holy Spirit. From the moment we are born again, God's Spirit supplies the power we need to be a consistent witness for Christ.

LESSON 1

WHO IS THE HOLY SPIRIT?

1. Who is the Holy Spirit?

John 14:16 _____

John 14:17 _____

2. What are some ways the Holy Spirit helps the believer?

Matthew 10:19–20 _____

John 14:26 _____

John 16:13–14 _____

Acts 1:8

Romans 8:14

Romans 8:15

Romans 8:16

Romans 8:26–27

2 Timothy 1:14

When we receive Christ as Savior and Lord, we are born again—that is, we are "born of the Spirit" (John 3:8).

Application & Reflection

What did you learn from this lesson? How will you apply it to your life?

LESSON 2

THE FRUIT OF THE SPIRIT

Fruitfulness is an important theme in the Bible. Jesus' picture in John 15:1-8 of how a grapevine is maintained is at the heart of Christ's teaching on our spiritual lives. These vines were not left alone on the ground to be trampled and to grow wild. A fruitful vine was lifted off the ground and constantly cared for by an attentive gardener. It would be absurd to think of a branch growing separately from the vine or a vine being fruitful and beautiful without constant help from the gardener.

1. How can we bring glory to the Father (John 15:8)?

2. What happens to the branches that do not bear fruit (John 15:2)?

_____

3. What happens to the branches that bear fruit (John 15:2)?

_____

_____

4. Why does the Father prune fruitful branches (John 15:2)?

_____

5. Can we bear fruit by ourselves (John 15:4)?

_____

6. What must we do to bear spiritual fruit (John 15:4–5)?

_____

7. What does it mean to "remain in the vine" (John 15:4–7)?

_____

_____

Jesus said that if we remain in him, we will "bear fruit." But what does this mean? Not long after Jesus' resurrection, the apostle Paul described what kind of fruit a Spirit-led, obedient life produces.

8. What are the fruit of the Spirit (Galatians 5:22–23)?

_____

_____

9. Which is the greatest (1 Corinthians 13:13)?

_____

10. Where does the Holy Spirit dwell (1 Corinthians 3:16)?

_____

God's Holy Spirit no longer dwells in buildings of brick and stone; he dwells in people! *We* are God's temple, and we show that we are his temple when we practice the fruit of the Spirit. The *you* in 1 Corinthians 3:16 is plural. Maybe that's because it's hard to practice virtues like love, peace, patience, and kindness on our own.

Application & Reflection

Do you see evidence of the fruit of the Spirit in your life? Which ones do you have? Which ones do you still need to develop?

_____

_____

_____

_____

LESSON 3

SPIRITUAL GIFTS

The *fruit* of the Spirit puts God's *character* on display (love, joy, peace, patience, etc.). The *gifts* of the Spirit put God's *power* on display. As his representatives on earth, we need to develop both. The fruit and the gifts of the Spirit were given for the common good—so that each of us can help build up the body of Christ.

1. What are the "spiritual gifts" that Paul mentions (Romans 12:6–8)?

   _____

   _____

2. What are the leadership gifts that God has placed in the church (Ephesians 4:11–12)?

   _____

   _____

3. What are the "manifestations of the Spirit" that are given for the common good (1 Corinthians 12:4–11)?

4. What attitude should we have regarding spiritual gifts (1 Corinthians 14:1)?

5. What should be our motivation for desiring and using our spiritual gifts (1 Corinthians 13:1–2)?

Read 1 Corinthians 14.

6. What does Paul say about the gift of prophecy (1 Corinthians 14)?

verse 1

verse 3

verse 4

verse 31

verses 39–40

7. What does Paul say about the gift of tongues (1 Corinthians 14)?

verse 2

verse 4

verse 5

verse 13

verse 14

verse 15

verses 39–40

8. What are we warned not to do?

1 Thessalonians 5:19–20 _____

Ephesians 4:30 _____

9. What did Jesus promise would happen to the disciples when the Holy Spirit came on them (Acts 1:8)?

_____

Application & Reflection

Have you experienced the Spirit's power in your life? How? What did you learn from this lesson? How will you apply it to your life?

_____

_____

_____

_____

LESSON 4

THE BAPTISM IN THE HOLY SPIRIT

1. What did John the Baptist promise Jesus would do (Matthew 3:11)?

_____

2. How did Peter describe the Gentiles' encounter with the Holy Spirit (Acts 11:15–17)?

_____

3. What did Jesus tell his disciples they were to do after he ascended to heaven?

Luke 24:49 _____

Acts 1:4–5 _____

4. Read the following five accounts of people who received the Holy Spirit in the book of Acts. How did they receive the Spirit? What happened when they received God's Spirit?

Acts 2:1–6 _____

Acts 8:14–19 _____

Acts 9:17–19 _____

Acts 10:44–48 _____

Acts 19:1–6 _____

5. Who does the Father give the Holy Spirit to (Luke 11:13)?

_____

Application & Reflection

Have you asked to receive God's Holy Spirit? What did you learn from this lesson? How will you apply it to your life?

_____

_____

_____

_____

_____

CHAPTER FIVE

SPIRITUAL HUNGER & GOD'S WORD

Oh, how I love your law! I meditate on it all day long.
Your commands are always with me. . . .
Your word is a lamp for my feet, a light on my path. . . .
I have put my hope in your word.

DAVID, PSALM 119:97-98, 105, 114

"Man shall not live on bread alone, but on every word that
comes from the mouth of God."

JESUS, MATTHEW 4:4

The Bible is more than an instruction manual or a rulebook. It is more than a random collection of stories, poems, and letters. It is the voice of God communicating with us. That is why the Bible is often referred to as "the Word of God."

In Psalm 119, the Israelite king David shows us how we should approach the Bible. David saw God's word as his source of life and hope. He delighted in it. He continually meditated on it. He understood that God spoke to him through it.

The bottom line? We know the sound of God's voice in our lives when we read his Word.

LESSON 1

THE AUTHORITY AND POWER OF THE WORD

"The word of God" is a big concept to grasp. And no simple, one-line definition will suffice. As you'll see in this lesson, the Bible refers to "God's word" as the driving force behind the creation of the universe. It's also a term Christians use to describe the Bible.

Sometimes "the word of God" refers in a more general sense to God's message of salvation that the first followers of Jesus proclaimed to the world (for example, Acts 6:7 and 8:14). And sometimes "the Word" refers to a person, as it does in John 1:14. In that amazing passage, we discover that *Jesus* is God's word to us.

The foundation of any healthy relationship is communication. God's word—in all its fullness—is his way of communicating with us.

1. How does the Bible say the world was created (2 Peter 3:5)?

   _____

   _____

2. What were the first followers of Jesus–his disciples–devoted to (Acts 2:42)?

   _____

   _____

3. What were the top two priorities for the early church leaders (Acts 6:4)?

_____

4. What happened as "the word of God" spread (Acts 6:7)?

_____

_____

5. What was "the word of the Lord" doing in Ephesus while Paul was there (Acts 19:20)?

_____

_____

6. How were the Scriptures originally given to us?

1 Corinthians 2:13 _____

2 Timothy 3:16 _____

7. What does John say about "the Word" (John 1:1)?

_____

_____

8. Who is "the Word" (John 1:14)?

_____

_____

9. What do the following passages teach about God's word?

Psalm 119:89 _____

Psalm 119:160 _____

Isaiah 40:8 _____

Isaiah 55:11 _____

Matthew 24:35 _____

John 17:17 _____

10. What does the writer of Hebrews say about God's word (Hebrews 4:12)?

_____

_____

_____

11. What does Jesus say we will be judged according to on the last day (John 12:48)?

_____

_____

_____

Application & Reflection

What does God's word mean to you? Spend some time reflecting on this today.

_____

_____

_____

_____

_____

LESSON 2

THE BENEFITS OF THE WORD

1. What was God's command to Joshua? What was his promise if Joshua obeyed (Joshua 1:8)?

_____

_____

2. How does the Bible describe the person who meditates on God's word (Psalm 1:1-3)?

_____

_____

3. What are the Scriptures useful for (2 Timothy 3:16-17)?

4. How did Jesus overcome temptation and defeat the devil (Matthew 4:1-11)?

The idea is not that having a few "magical" memory verses will get us out of any situation. Rather, it's that when we meditate on the Scriptures, turning to them for strength and guidance becomes second nature—as it was for Jesus when the devil tempted him.

5. How can God's people experience victory over sin?

Psalm 119:9
Psalm 119:11

6. What are some of the ways God's word benefits the believer?

Psalm 119:98–100
Psalm 119:105
Psalm 119:165
Proverbs 4:20–22

Application & Reflection
What did you learn from this lesson? How will you apply it to your life?

LESSON 3

SPIRITUAL HUNGER

If someone is deprived of food and water for an extended period of time, his or her physical body will weaken and eventually die. There is a spiritual parallel. The word of God is our spiritual food and water. As surely as we will die physically without food and water, we will die spiritually without God's word.

1. What was David's greatest desire (Psalm 119:81)?

2. How did the sons of Korah describe the condition of their souls (Psalm 42:1-2)?

3. What was the psalmist's attitude toward God's presence (Psalm 84:1-2, 10)?

4. Who did Jesus say will be "filled" (Matthew 5:6)?

5. What do you think it means to "hunger and thirst for righteousness" (Matthew 5:6)?

6. What did David say about God's word and its importance in his life?

   Psalm 119:72

   Psalm 119:103

   Psalm 119:127

7. How would you describe Job's hunger for God's word (Job 23:12)?

8. What did Jeremiah say about God's word (Jeremiah 15:16)?

Application & Reflection

What did you learn from this lesson? How will you apply it to your life?

LESSON 4

OBEDIENCE

1. What happens if we only *listen* to the word (James 1:22)?

2. How does James describe those who only listen to the word without putting it into practice (James 1:23–24)?

3. What happens to those who hear and act on the word (James 1:25)?

4. How did the Bereans respond to the preaching of Paul and Silas? How often did they read and study the Scriptures (Acts 17:11)?

5. If we call Jesus our Lord, what should we do (Luke 6:46–49)?

6. What happens to the person who hears Jesus' words and puts them into practice (Luke 6:46–48)?

7. What happens to the person who hears Jesus' words but does not put them into practice (Luke 6:49)?

8. If we hold to Jesus' teaching, what will happen (John 8:31–32)?

9. What is the proof of our love for Jesus (John 14:21, 23–24)?

Application & Reflection

What did you learn from this lesson? How will you apply it to your life?

CHAPTER SIX

DISCIPLESHIP & LEADERSHIP

Jesus went out and saw a tax collector by the name of Levi sitting at his tax booth. "Follow me," Jesus said to him, and Levi got up, left everything and followed him.

LUKE 5:27-28

"Whoever wants to be my disciple must deny themselves and take up their cross daily and follow me. For whoever wants to save their life will lose it, but whoever loses their life for me will save it."

JESUS, LUKE 9:23-24

Follow my example, as I follow the example of Christ.

PAUL, 1 CORINTHIANS 11:1

Jesus calls us to "go and make disciples of all nations" (Matthew 28:19). This charge propelled the early followers of Christ into a strategic mission that turned the world upside down—not just by preaching the gospel, but by training the new believers as well. To be a Christian is to be a disciple—a lifelong learner and follower of Jesus.

LESSON 1

THE CALL: MAKE DISCIPLES

1. What did Jesus call his followers to do (Matthew 28:19)?

2. What did Jesus say they must do after baptizing a new believer (Matthew 28:20)?

3. As the word of God spread in first century Jerusalem, what was the result (Acts 6:7)?

4. What did Paul command Timothy to do with the things he had been taught (2 Timothy 2:2)?

Read 2 Timothy 2:3–6. In these verses, Paul compares the life of a disciple to the life of a soldier, an athlete, and a farmer. He then promises that if Timothy will reflect on these things, the Lord will give him insight.

5. What does each of these illustrations teach you about discipleship?

Soldier: _____

Athlete: _____

Farmer: _____

6. What are the Scriptures useful for (2 Timothy 3:16)?

_____

_____

7. How did Jesus say we can know we are truly his disciples (John 8:31)?

_____

8. How can disciples become like their teacher (Luke 6:40)?

_____

9. How does Jesus describe the person who hears his teaching and acts on it (Luke 6:48)?

_____

_____

10. How does he describe the person who hears and does *not* act on his teaching (Luke 6:49)?

_____

_____

Jesus compares those who put his words into practice to a man who dug down deep and laid a foundation on the rock. This is the most critical part of any house. It is why you, as a disciple, must lay a strong spiritual foundation. These Bible studies are intended to do just that—to help you lay the foundation for the Christian life. If you are discipling someone else, you have the opportunity to help that person lay the foundation for a never-ending relationship with Jesus Christ.

11. What has Christ called us to? Why has he called us to do this (2 Timothy 1:9)?

_____

12. What does the Bible say about those who are "in Christ" (2 Corinthians 5:17)?

_____

We are called to a whole new life. We are not only forgiven of our sins but are also given new hearts. And our new hearts will yearn to follow Christ.

Application & Reflection
In your own words, what do you think it means to be a disciple?

_____
_____
_____
_____

LESSON 2

THE COST: ABSOLUTE SURRENDER
1. What three things did Jesus say all his disciples must do (Mark 8:34)?

_____
_____

2. How often should someone who wants to be a disciple take up their cross (Luke 9:23)?

_____

Taking up your cross is the ultimate act of surrender—a conscious choice to deny yourself and live for Christ. It means a willingness to follow and obey Christ to whatever end.

3. How did Jesus compare discipleship to a war (Luke 14:31–33)?

_____

_____

4. What else did Jesus compare being a disciple to (Luke 14:28)?

_____

_____

5. What should we do before we start "building" (Luke 14:28–33)?

_____

6. What does it mean to count the cost of being a disciple?

_____

_____

7. What has it cost you to follow Jesus? What are you willing to give up in order to follow him?

_____

_____

8. When it comes to discipleship, why is it so important to be able to finish what we start (Luke 14:29–30)?

_____

_____

9. Who cannot be a disciple (Luke 14:27, 33)?

_____

_____

It is critical to understand what is being said here, as well as what is not being said. God has called us into his kingdom through his grace. Being "born again" (John 3:3) means that we have new life. Although salvation is a free gift, it costs us everything.

Make no mistake: *we cannot buy God's love and forgiveness*. But Jesus doesn't beat around the bush: it will cost us everything to follow him. If we want to be Jesus' disciples, we can have no other gods before him.

Application & Reflection
What did you learn from this lesson? How will you apply it to your life?

_____

_____

_____

_____

LESSON 3

DISCIPLESHIP AND THE CROSS
There is a difference between the cross of Christ and the cross we pick up when we become his disciples. Because of Christ's victory on the cross, we are freed from sin and made "slaves" of righteousness (Romans 6:17–18). Jesus gives us the power to pick up our cross and follow him.

1. What happened at the cross (Colossians 2:13–15)?

   _____

   _____

2. How did Paul describe his message to the Corinthians (1 Corinthians 2:1–2)?

   _____

3. What is the message of the cross to the perishing? What about to those who are being saved (1 Corinthians 1:18)?

   _____

   _____

The cross is "foolishness" to those who are perishing because it destroys self-effort. We marvel at the greatness of God's work in paying our sin debt and delivering us from the power of evil.

4. What did Paul boast in (Galatians 6:14)?

_____

Paul had previously bragged about his religious accomplishments. But after encountering the cross, he could only brag about what Christ did for him, not what he supposedly did for God.

5. What happened in Paul's life as a result of Jesus' death on the cross (Galatians 6:14)?

_____

_____

6. What do you think Paul meant when he said, "I have been crucified with Christ" (Galatians 2:20)?

_____

_____

7. What did he mean by the phrase, "I no longer live, but Christ lives in me" (Galatians 2:20)?

_____

_____

Application & Reflection
What do you think it means for you to be crucified with Christ?

_____

_____

_____

_____

LESSON 4

CHRISTIAN CHARACTER

Those who are disciples will show it through their lives. It is critical that we cultivate the fruit of a godly life as we follow Christ in discipleship. Read 2 Peter 1:3–11.

1. What has God provided for us by his divine power (2 Peter 1:3)?

2. How are we able to "participate in the divine nature" (2 Peter 1:4)?

3. What can we escape as a result (2 Peter 1:4)?

The most important mark of a disciple of Jesus Christ is not charisma, but godly character. We should never minimize the importance of the gifts of the Holy Spirit, yet it is the fruit of the Spirit that identifies the true follower of Jesus. When Jesus was teaching his disciples how to identify false prophets, he said, "By their fruit you will recognize them" (Matthew 7:19–20).

Many are gifted, yet the real test is a person's character, habits, and lifestyle. Although every disciple is given gifts for the benefit of the entire body of Christ, it is the fruit of a godly life that we must cultivate if we are to bear the marks of a true follower of Jesus.

Charisma is important. Character is essential.

4. What is the foundational "ingredient" to which everything else needed for a godly life is added (2 Peter 1:5)?

5. What are the necessary "additives" that Peter lists (2 Peter 1:5-7)?

6. What is the promised result of having these qualities in "increasing measure" (2 Peter 1:8)?

7. What is the condition of those without these character qualities (2 Peter 1:9)?

8. What is the promise to those who develop this Christian character (2 Peter 1:10-11)?

9. Why should we rejoice in suffering (Romans 5:3-4)?

10. Why did James say we could consider trials "pure joy" (James 1:2-3)?

11. What results in our lives when perseverance finishes its work (James 1:4)?

The process of spiritual maturity and Christian character development can be summarized as follows:

James 1:2–4	Trials and testing of faith ➤ Perseverance ➤ Maturity
Romans 5:3–4	Suffering ➤ Perseverance ➤ Character

Application & Reflection
What did you learn from this lesson? How will you apply it to your life?

_____

_____

_____

_____

LESSON 5

DISCIPLESHIP AND LEADERSHIP
Jesus' original disciples became great leaders. Their lives and message impacted the world. But they didn't start out as leaders. They started as disciples. Anyone who wants to lead first has to learn how to follow (Luke 22:26–27).

1. What did Jesus tell his first disciples to do (Matthew 4:19)?

_____

2. What did Jesus promise he would do for his followers if they responded (Matthew 4:19)?

_____

3. How did the first disciples respond to Jesus' command and promise (Matthew 4:20)?

_____

After a season of intense personal discipleship, Jesus sent his followers out on their own to practice what they had watched him do.

4. What did Jesus give his disciples authority to do (Matthew 10:1)?

_____

_____

5. What did they do with that authority (Mark 6:7, 12–13)?

_____

_____

6. Did Jesus want his disciples just to follow him and watch him minister, or did he want them to watch, learn, and do all they saw him do?

_____

_____

The central call to discipleship is learning to follow Jesus ourselves, as well as helping others in this process.

7. Are you in a discipleship group? Who is the leader? When and where does the group meet?

_____

_____

Read Matthew 28:18–20.

8. What did Jesus tell his discipleship group before he left earth (Matthew 28:19)?

_____

9. What are we to teach the people we are discipling (Matthew 28:20)?

_____

10. What is the difference between teaching facts and teaching someone to obey God's commands (Matthew 28:20)?

_____

_____

11. What was Jesus' final promise to all who attempt to make disciples (Matthew 28:20)?

_____

Discipleship is foundational to Christianity, but at its core, it's a simple concept. In fact, it's so simple that 2,000 years ago Jesus explained it to a group of fishermen in one sentence: "Come, follow me . . . and I will send you out to fish for people" (Matthew 4:19). To be a disciple is to follow Jesus, reach the lost, and engage in this process with other believers.

Application & Reflection
What did you learn from this lesson? How will you apply it to your life?

_____

_____

_____

_____

CHAPTER SEVEN

SPIRITUAL FAMILY & CHURCH LIFE

"I will build my church, and the gates of Hades will not overcome it."

JESUS, MATTHEW 16:18

They devoted themselves to the apostles' teaching and to fellowship, to the breaking of bread and to prayer. Everyone was filled with awe at the many wonders and signs performed by the apostles. All the believers were together and had everything in common. They sold property and possessions to give to anyone who had need. Every day they continued to meet together in the temple courts. They broke bread in their homes and ate together with glad and sincere hearts, praising God and enjoying the favor of all the people. And the Lord added to their number daily those who were being saved.

ACTS 2:42-47

There is one body and one Spirit . . . one Lord, one faith, one baptism; one God and Father of all.

EPHESIANS 4:4-6

Peter preached the very first sermon of the New Testament church. He called his listeners to repent, to be baptized, and to receive the Holy Spirit. All who responded were then added to the local body of believers—called the *church*. Everyone who is saved, baptized, and filled with the Holy Spirit today should also become part of a church—a local community of believers.

Why? Because we were not made to live the Christian life alone. We were not meant to follow God by ourselves. As you'll discover in this study, the early church did nearly everything in community. They didn't just meet together once a week; they shared life together. They taught one another, encouraged one another, and met each other's needs.

Just as God determines our parents and other family members, he has also chosen the spiritual family that we are born into. The church is God's instrument for advancing his kingdom. He has no "plan B." The church is the only legitimate setting for living the Christian faith. No long-term "lone ranger" can be a true disciple of Christ. All who truly desire to follow Christ must find their place in a church family.

LESSON 1

THE VICTORIOUS CHURCH

1. What did Jesus say about his victorious church (Matthew 16:18)?

2. Who is the "rock" (1 Corinthians 10:4)?

3. Who is the "chief cornerstone" (Ephesians 2:20)?

4. What does Paul compare the love Christ has for the church to (Ephesians 5:25-28)?

5. How does Paul describe the ultimate destiny of the church (Ephesians 5:26-27)?

6. What were the first church members devoted to (Acts 2:42)?

7. How would you describe early church life (Acts 2:42-47)?

verse 43

verse 44

verse 45

verse 46

verse 47

8. How would you describe the generosity of the early church (Acts 4:32-37)?

Application & Reflection

Are you part of a church community? If so, how is your church similar to the one described in Acts 2:43-47 and 4:32-37? How is it different? What can you learn from the early church?

LESSON 2

THE BODY OF CHRIST

1. What does Paul call the people of God (1 Corinthians 12:27)?

The Bible says the church is the "body of Christ" and that each person is like a different part of the body, with something unique to offer. That's why belonging to a church community is such a vital part of following Jesus. When we "go it alone," we're not only hurting ourselves but also hurting the body of Christ. It's like cutting off a finger or pulling out an eye.

2. What does Paul say about the importance of each part of the body of Christ (1 Corinthians 12:14–20)?

3. Who decides how each part of the body should function (1 Corinthians 12:18)?

4. What does Paul say to those who think they do not need the rest of the body (1 Corinthians 12:21)?

5. What does Paul say about the parts of the body "that seem to be weaker" (1 Corinthians 12:22–24)?

6. How should the different parts of the body treat each other (1 Corinthians 12:25–26)?

The Bible puts a lot of importance on the diversity of the church—many different people from all walks of life who bring different gifts and talents to the body of Christ. Yet equally important is an unshakable unity that comes from having Jesus Christ as our common foundation.

7. What are the seven "ones" mentioned in Ephesians 4:4-6?

One _____

One _____

One _____

One _____

One _____

One _____

One _____

8. What should we do to maintain oneness or unity (Ephesians 4:3)?

_____

_____

9. What did Jesus pray for regarding the unity of his disciples (John 17:20-21)?

_____

_____

10. What does the Bible call someone who stirs up dissension—that is, who causes *dis*unity (Proverbs 16:28)?

_____

_____

Read Proverbs 6:16-19.

11. This passage lists seven things that are "detestable" to the Lord. What is the seventh (Proverbs 6:19)?

_____

Application & Reflection

What role do you believe God is calling you to serve in his church? How has he gifted you? Try asking a Christian friend who knows you well what he or she thinks your gifts may be.

_____

_____

_____

_____

LESSON 3

CHURCH LEADERSHIP

The early church was not merely an organization but also a living organism powered by God's Holy Spirit. That's the way the church today should be. Still, without some organization and structure, even a Spirit-led movement can turn into chaos.

The early church in Jerusalem gives a perfect example of this truth (Acts 6:1–7). Every day, the believers distributed food to the widows in their community. (In the first century world, widows had little or no means of support.) But some of the widows were being overlooked.

The twelve apostles—the leaders of the early church—knew they could not address important logistical issues while keeping their focus on "the ministry of the word of God." So they appointed several others to care for the widows. This is a compelling picture of different people with different gifts serving the body of Christ in different ways.

1. What five roles of authority and leadership did God place in the church (Ephesians 4:11)?

   _____

   _____

SPIRITUAL FAMILY & CHURCH LIFE

2. What is the job of these leaders (Ephesians 4:12–13)?

   _____

3. How long will these gifts operate in the church (Ephesians 4:13)?

   _____

4. What is the result of being in a church where these five ministries are operating (Ephesians 4:14)?

   _____

   _____

5. How is the body of Christ "joined and held together" (Ephesians 4:16)?

   _____

   _____

Read Titus 1:5–9 and 1 Timothy 3:1–7.

6. Why was Titus left in Crete (Titus 1:5)?

   _____

   _____

7. What are the qualifications for being an elder (Titus 1:6–9; 1 Timothy 3:2–7)?

   _____

   _____

8. What do these passages teach about an elder's marriage, children, and home life?

   _____

   _____

9. What was Peter's exhortation to the elders (1 Peter 5:1–4)?

   _____

   _____

Application & Reflection

What did you learn from this lesson? How will you apply it to your life?

_____

_____

_____

_____

LESSON 4

CHURCH DISCIPLINE

1. What are some of the responsibilities of pastors, elders, and spiritual leaders?

John 21:15–17 _____

Acts 20:28 _____

Ezekiel 33:1–9 _____

Ezekiel 34:2–5 _____

2. How should church members relate to their pastors, their elders, and their spiritual leaders?

1 Thessalonians 5:12–13 _____

1 Thessalonians 5:25 _____

1 Timothy 5:17–18 _____

Hebrews 13:7 _____

Hebrews 13:17 _____

3. Who is the "head" of the church (Ephesians 4:15)?

_____

4. What is the "foundation" of the church (1 Corinthians 3:10–11)?

_____

The church is meant to be a community of people who are helping each other grow closer to God. In other words, the process of sanctification, which we covered in chapter 2, is not something we can do on our own.

In any community, people will eventually offend one another or let one another down. The church is no exception. The good news is that the Bible offers a road map for responding to offense, sin, and division within the church. Sometimes this road map is referred to as "church discipline" or "accountability." But the goal is always the same: to encourage repentance, healing, and restoration.

5. What should we do if we know a brother or sister has something against us (Matthew 5:23–24)?

6. What three steps should be taken to deal with sin in the church (Matthew 18:15–17)?

verse 15

verse 16

verse 17

7. What should happen to the church member who is consistently wicked and immoral (1 Corinthians 5:9–13)?

8. If we have no discipline, what are we (Hebrews 12:8)?

9. What will we share in as a result of this discipline (Hebrews 12:10)?

10. What will this discipline ultimately produce (Hebrews 12:11)?

_____

_____

Application & Reflection

What did you learn from this lesson? How will you apply it to your life?

_____

_____

_____

_____

LESSON 5

HOLY COMMUNION

The night before Jesus was executed, he shared one last meal with his disciples. During the meal, he took some bread, tore it into pieces, and passed it around the table. He told his disciples to take and eat the bread. "This is my body," he said. Moments later he passed around a cup, telling them each to drink, saying, "This is my blood of the covenant, which is poured out for many for the forgiveness of sins" (Matthew 26:26, 28).

Jesus told his disciples to eat and drink in remembrance of him. This "communion," as it is often called, represents Jesus' sacrifice on the cross—as well as our new life and new relationship with him. To this day, followers of Jesus observe "communion" in obedience to him.

1. What were the early disciples devoted to (Acts 2:42)?

_____

_____

SPIRITUAL FAMILY & CHURCH LIFE

Read 1 Corinthians 11:23–32.

2. What is proclaimed when we have communion (1 Corinthians 11:26)?

_____

_____

_____

3. What are we guilty of if we receive communion in an "unworthy manner" (1 Corinthians 11:27)?

_____

_____

4. What should we do before we receive communion (1 Corinthians 11:28)?

_____

_____

5. What happens to us if we continue to receive communion and do not turn from sin (1 Corinthians 11:29)?

_____

_____

6. What can happen as a result of this (1 Corinthians 11:30)?

_____

_____

7. How can we avoid being judged (1 Corinthians 11:31)?

_____

_____

8. When God judges or disciplines his children, what is his motive (1 Corinthians 11:32)?

_____

_____

Application & Reflection

What did you learn from this lesson? How will you apply it to your life?

_____

_____

_____

_____

_____

CHAPTER EIGHT

PRAYER & WORSHIP

Rejoice in the Lord always. I will say it again: Rejoice! . . .
The Lord is near. Do not be anxious about anything, but in
every situation, by prayer and petition, with thanksgiving,
present your requests to God.

PAUL, PHILIPPIANS 4:4, 5B-6

I want the men everywhere to pray, lifting up holy hands without
anger or disputing.

PAUL, 1 TIMOTHY 2:8

The prayer of a righteous person is powerful and effective.

JAMES 5:16

Christianity is more than just a religion. It is a relationship between
God and humanity. All relationships grow through communication.

The better the communication, the better the relationship will be. Communication is a two-way process involving both talking and listening. God talks to us in many ways but primarily through his Word. We talk to him through prayer and worship. We listen to him as we read the Bible. He listens to us when we pray and worship. We respond to his Word with action. He responds to our prayers and worship with action.

LESSON 1

PERSONAL PRAYER

By observing Jesus' personal prayer life, we find two keys to effective prayer: a specific time and a private place.

1. When and where did Jesus pray (Mark 1:35)?

2. Where do the hypocrites pray (Matthew 6:5)?

3. Where did Jesus teach his followers to pray (Matthew 6:6)?

To the hypocrites of Jesus' day, prayer was a form of spiritual one-upmanship, a way of showing off in front of others. Jesus taught that prayer should be an intimate time of connection with the Father, not a time for impressing others with our religious vocabulary.

4. To whom did Jesus say we should pray (Matthew 6:6, 8–9)?

_____

_____

_____

The fact that we can call God our "Father" when we pray is nothing
short of amazing. The Old Testament taught that God was a Father
to his people (Deuteronomy 32:6; Isaiah 63:16; Malachi 2:10), but
before Jesus, virtually no one addressed God as their "Father" when
they prayed. Jesus brings us into a new level of relationship with God.
Through Jesus, God adopts us and becomes our Father.

5. What do the pagans think about prayer (Matthew 6:7)?

_____

_____

_____

6. What should we pray for (Matthew 6:9–13)?

verse 9 _____

verse 10 _____

verse 11 _____

verse 12 _____

verse 13 _____

Application & Reflection

Think about the role prayer plays in your own life. Do you have specific time set
aside for daily prayer? When? Do you have a private place for prayer? Where?

_____

_____

_____

_____

LESSON 2

THE POWER OF PRAYER

1. What does Jesus promise to those who ask, seek, and knock (Matthew 7:7–11)?

2. What does Jesus say we must do for our prayers to be answered (Mark 11:24)?

3. What can we receive if we pray and believe (Matthew 21:22)?

4. What might be a reason we don't receive what we ask for (James 4:3)?

5. What does Jesus teach about prayer in the parable of the persistent widow? Why did he tell the parable (Luke 18:1–8)?

6. What can hinder our prayers?

   Psalm 66:18–19

   James 1:6–8

   1 Peter 3:7

7. In whose name should we pray (John 14:12-14)?

8. Who should we present our requests to (Philippians 4:6)?

9. How do we get to God (John 14:6)?

10. How many mediators are there between God and us? Who is the mediator (1 Timothy 2:5)?

11. What is the confidence we have in prayer (1 John 5:14–15)?

12. What were the results of the disciples' prayers (Acts 4:31)?

13. What were Paul and Silas doing while in prison (Acts 16:25)?

14. What were the results of their prayers (Acts 16:26–34)?

15. What was Elijah's prayer request and God's answer (James 5:17–18)?

Application & Reflection

What did you learn from this lesson about the power of prayer? How has God answered your own prayers?

_____

_____

_____

_____

_____

LESSON 3

CORPORATE PRAYER

In the first lesson, we learned the importance of personal prayer and were cautioned about praying in public simply to be seen by others as "spiritual." However, we are encouraged to pray together as Christians.

1. What were the disciples doing as they waited for the day of Pentecost and the outpouring of the Holy Spirit (Acts 1:13–14)?

_____

_____

2. What did the believers do when they heard of Peter and John's arrest and persecution at the hands of the Sanhedrin (Acts 4:23–24)?

_____

_____

3. In the midst of persecution, what were their prayer requests (Acts 4:29–30)?

_____

_____

_____

4. What was the church doing while Peter was in prison (Acts 12:5, 12)?

5. How did God answer their prayers (Acts 12:7–12)?

6. What were the Antioch church leaders doing when God called Saul and Barnabas to the mission field (Acts 13:2)?

7. What did they do before sending them off (Acts 13:3)?

8. What is essential in corporate prayer (Matthew 18:19)?

9. What did Jesus promise (Matthew 18:20)?

Application & Reflection

What did you learn from this lesson? How will you apply it to your life? Do you have a community of believers with whom you can pray regularly?

LESSON 4

A BIBLICAL PRAYER LIST

1. What was Paul's prayer for the disciples in Ephesus?

   Ephesians 1:17 _____

   Ephesians 1:18 _____

   Ephesians 3:16 _____

   Ephesians 3:17–19 _____

2. What was Paul's prayer for the Philippian church (Philippians 1:9–11)?

3. What was Paul's prayer for the Colossians (Colossians 1:9–12)?

4. What did Paul instruct the Colossians to pray for (Colossians 4:2–4)?

5. What was Epaphras always doing for the Colossians (Colossians 4:12)?

6. What was Paul's prayer request to the Thessalonian believers (2 Thessalonians 3:1–2)?

7. What was Paul's prayer for Philemon (Philemon 4–6)?

Application & Reflection
What did you learn from this lesson? How will you apply it to your life? What does your prayer list look like compared to the lists of Paul and the early believers?

LESSON 5

WORSHIP

1. What kind of people is God seeking (John 4:23)?

2. How should we worship God (John 4:24)?

3. Our worship is to be in the Spirit and in truth. What does God say about the use of physical idols, statues, and images in worship (Deuteronomy 5:8–10)?

4. What are we encouraged not to do (Hebrews 10:24–25)?

5. What internal attitudes make our worship acceptable to God (Hebrews 12:28–29)?

6. What are some external expressions of worship encouraged in Scripture?

Psalm 47:1, 5–6 _____

Psalm 96:8–9 _____

Psalm 98:1, 4–6 _____

Psalm 149:3 _____

Psalm 150:3–6 _____

7. In what two places did the early church meet for worship and prayer?

Acts 2:46 _____

Acts 20:20 _____

Application & Reflection

What did you learn from this lesson? How will you apply it to your life? In what ways do you express your love for God?

_____

_____

_____

_____

_____

CHAPTER NINE

FAITH & HOPE

*Now faith is confidence in what we hope for and assurance
about what we do not see.*

HEBREWS 11:1

*[God] took [Abram] outside and said, "Look up at the sky and
count the stars—if indeed you can count them." Then he said
to him, "So shall your offspring be." Abram believed the LORD,
and he credited it to him as righteousness.*

GENESIS 15:5–6

"The righteous will live by faith."

ROMANS 1:17

In chapter 1 we learned that we are saved by grace through faith (Ephesians 2:8). But that's only the beginning. Once we become followers of Jesus, we continue to live each day by faith in the one who saved us.

LESSON 1

WHAT IS FAITH?

Hebrews 11 paints an extraordinary picture of faith, telling story after story of men and women who put their faith in God and demonstrated their faith by obeying him, often at great cost to themselves.

1. Faith is one of the few words that the Bible defines for us. What is faith (Hebrews 11:1)?

2. How does faith come to us (Romans 10:17)?

3. How does faith express itself (Galatians 5:6)?

4. What do the following verses teach about faith?

   Galatians 2:16
   Galatians 3:11
   Galatians 3:26

5. What is the foundation that must be laid in the life of every believer who wants to go on to maturity (Hebrews 6:1–2)?

6. Who are we to put our faith in (Galatians 2:16)?

After the resurrection, Thomas (one of the disciples) refused to believe Jesus was alive unless he saw it for himself. He stubbornly told the other disciples, "Unless I see the nail marks in his hands and put my finger where the nails were, and put my hand into his side, I will not believe" (John 20:25). Only when Jesus finally appeared did Thomas believe.

7. After Thomas finally believed, who did Jesus say would be blessed (John 20:29)?

8. What should we do when our senses contradict our faith (2 Corinthians 5:7)?

Application & Reflection

What are some things you are certain of but do not see (e.g., air, North Pole, God)?

LESSON 2

SAVING FAITH

Read Acts 16:16–34.

1. What did Paul and Silas tell the jailer he had to do to be saved (Acts 16:30–31)?

2. What did Paul tell the Romans they needed to do to be saved (Romans 10:9–10)?

3. How are we justified (Romans 5:1)?

_____

To be "justified" is to be made right with God. Our sin (and the punishment for it) is taken away, and God declares us to be "righteous"—that is, to be in a right relationship with him.

4. What is the result of our justification (Romans 5:1)?

_____

_____

5. How can we have access to God's grace (Romans 5:1-2)?

_____

Read Romans 3:21-28.

6. Are people justified before God by obeying the law or by putting their faith in God (Romans 3:28)?

_____

7. Who does God justify (Romans 3:26)?

_____

8. How does righteousness come (Romans 3:22)?

_____

9. How do the righteous live (Romans 1:17)?

_____

10. Paul spoke of a righteousness that did not come from the law. Where did it come from (Philippians 3:8-9)?

_____

_____

11. How are we saved (Ephesians 2:8)?

_____

12. Who has the right to become "children of God" (John 1:12)?

_____

13. Who will "not perish but have eternal life" (John 3:16)?

_____

Application & Reflection

What did you learn from this lesson? How will you apply it to your life?

_____

_____

_____

_____

LESSON 3

FAITH AND OBEDIENCE

Faith is more than a one-time mental acknowledgment of who Jesus is and what he has done for us. God wants those who have been saved to continue to live by faith; that is, he wants our faith to lead to faith*fulness* (Habakkuk 2:4; Romans 1:17; Galatians 2:20; 3:11; Hebrews 10:38).

1. What does James say about faith that is not accompanied by action (James 2:17)?

_____

2. Is just saying that we believe in God enough (James 2:19)?

_____

3. What are all people called to (Romans 1:5)?

_____

4. What did Abel do "by faith" (Hebrews 11:4)?

_____

5. God called Abraham to a place he had never seen. What did Abraham do "by faith" (Hebrews 11:8)?

_____

6. When God tested Abraham, what did he do "by faith" (Hebrews 11:17)?

_____

7. After growing up in the lap of luxury as the son of Pharaoh's daughter, what did Moses do "by faith"? What did he choose "by faith" (Hebrews 11:24-25)?

_____

_____

8. What else did Moses do "by faith" (Hebrews 11:27-28)?

_____

_____

9. What did all the Israelites do "by faith" (Hebrews 11:29)?

_____

10. What happened in Jericho because of the Israelites' obedient faith (Hebrews 11:30)?

_____

_____

11. Is it possible to be a man or woman of great faith and die without receiving what has been promised (Hebrews 11:37-39)?

_____

Obedience does not lead to salvation, but the Bible does teach that salvation—putting our faith in Jesus—leads to obedience.

12. What does it mean to love God (1 John 5:3)?

_____

13. Are God's commands a burden? Why or why not (1 John 5:3)?

_____

14. How does John describe faith (1 John 5:4)?

_____

_____

15. Who overcomes the world (1 John 5:5)?

_____

Application & Reflection

How has your faith in God led to faithfulness? What did you learn from this lesson? How will you apply it to your life?

_____

_____

_____

_____

LESSON 4

MOUNTAIN-MOVING FAITH

1. The disciples once failed to cast out a demon and asked Jesus, "Why couldn't we drive it out?" What was the reason they couldn't drive it out (Matthew 17:19-20)?

_____

2. Even if we have small faith in a big God, what can we do (Matthew 17:20)?

_____

There are two truths about God that serve as foundations for our faith. Abraham, the father of our faith, understood these faith foundations (Romans 4:16–17). To be men and women of faith, we must hold tightly to these two truths about God:

- God is powerful = God is able (Romans 4:18–21)
- God is faithful = God is willing (Hebrews 11:11)

3. What was Abraham fully persuaded of (Romans 4:21)?

_____

4. Some people ignore or deny the facts in a vain attempt to move in faith. What did Abraham do in regard to the physical facts (Romans 4:19)?

_____

5. What were the facts in Abraham's case (Romans 4:19)?

_____

6. What did Abraham *not* do when he faced the facts (Romans 4:20)?

_____

7. Why were Abraham and Sarah able to become parents (Hebrews 11:11)?

_____

8. What promise had God made to Abraham (Genesis 15:4–6)?

_____

9. In Ephesians 6:10–17, Paul calls believers to put on "the full armor of God." What can the "shield of faith" do (Ephesians 6:16)?

_____

10. Who should we have faith in (Mark 11:22)?

_____

11. What must we do if we want our "mountain" to be thrown "into the sea" (Mark 11:23)?

_____

_____

Application & Reflection

How have you seen the power of faith demonstrated in your own life? In the lives of others?

_____

_____

_____

_____

LESSON 5

FAITH AND HOPE

Faith and hope are closely related in the Bible. But biblical hope is much more than simply longing for something that *might* happen. It is a confident assurance—rooted in faith—that God will do what he has promised to do.

1. What must we believe about God in order to come to him (Hebrews 11:6)?

_____

_____

2. What is impossible without faith (Hebrews 11:6)?

3. What is the connection between faith and hope (Hebrews 11:1)?

4. What did the writer of Hebrews call hope (Hebrews 6:19)?

5. What is the purpose of an anchor in a boat?

6. How does hope anchor our soul? What happens to a person who has no hope?

7. Faith deals with today, while hope deals with tomorrow. What are we now by *faith* (1 John 3:2)?

8. What will happen to us when Jesus appears—that is, what is our *hope* (1 John 3:2)?

9. How should this hope of seeing Jesus affect our lives (1 John 3:3)?

Application & Reflection
What did you learn from this lesson? How will you apply it to your life?

CHAPTER TEN

BIBLICAL PROSPERITY & GENEROSITY

Remember this: Whoever sows sparingly will also reap sparingly, and whoever sows generously will also reap generously. Each of you should give what you have decided in your heart to give, not reluctantly or under compulsion, for God loves a cheerful giver. And God is able to bless you abundantly, so that in all things at all times, having all that you need, you will abound in every good work. . . . You will be enriched in every way so that you can be generous on every occasion.

PAUL, 2 CORINTHIANS 9:6-8, 11

Literally thousands of passages in the Bible deal with the subject of money. Money is a powerful tool that, like most things, can be used either for great good or for great evil. In this chapter, we will explore both the dangers and opportunities that money brings to a follower of Jesus. We will also examine our attitude toward money to see if we view money as means to an end or as an end in itself.

LESSON 1

THE DANGERS OF WEALTH

1. According to Jesus' parable of the sower, what can choke out God's word and cause it to be unfruitful (Mark 4:18–19)?

2. What are some ways that people are deceived by wealth?

3. What are some worries of life that choke out God's word (Matthew 6:25, 28, 31, 34)?

For most people in the first century, food, drink, and clothing were much more matters of life and death than they are for many today. So if Jesus told people back then not to worry about these things, how much more should we not succumb to the worries of life?

4. Who does Jesus say it is impossible to serve alongside God (Luke 16:13)?

Jesus never made such a statement about anything else. He did not say, "You cannot serve God and power . . . God and sin . . . God and career . . . God and self." Why not? Because people know instinctively they must serve God alone. However, because of the deceitful nature of money and wealth, many people are convinced they are serving God when they have actually become slaves to money.

5. What can happen to those who are eager for money and want to get rich (1 Timothy 6:9–10)?

6. Do you want to get rich? What are some potential dangers of this desire?

7. What is a root of all kinds of evil (1 Timothy 6:10)?

8. What can deliver us from death—righteousness or money (Proverbs 11:4)?

9. What happens to those who trust in money (Proverbs 11:28)?

10. Do riches last (Proverbs 23:4–5)?

11. What should we guard ourselves against (Luke 12:15)?

12. Read Luke 12:16–21. What is the point of the parable of the rich fool?

Application & Reflection
What did you learn about the dangers of money?

_____

_____

_____

_____

LESSON 2

BIBLICAL PRINCIPLES OF PROSPERITY

Having established the dangerous nature of money, we can now look at some of the positive things the Bible says about money, abundance, and prosperity. Just because something is dangerous doesn't mean we should never use it. For example, cars are dangerous, but that doesn't mean we should stop driving and walk everywhere. It simply means we need to obey traffic rules. In the same way, the proper response to the dangers of money is not to be intentionally poor but to handle the money God gives us according to his principles.

1. Who gives us the ability to produce wealth (Deuteronomy 8:18)?

   _____

2. Read Deuteronomy 30:8-10. What did Moses tell the Israelites God would do for them if they obeyed his commands?

   _____

3. What do the following verses from Proverbs have to say about prosperity, or God's provision?

   Proverbs 10:3 _____
   Proverbs 10:4 _____

Proverbs 10:22

Proverbs 13:21

Proverbs 13:22

Proverbs 21:21

Proverbs 22:4

Proverbs 22:9

4. What happens when we give? What if we give with small measure? What if we give with a large measure (Luke 6:38)?

5. How does the "law of sowing and reaping" apply to money (2 Corinthians 9:6)?

6. What kind of giver does God love (2 Corinthians 9:7)?

7. What is God able to do for the cheerful giver (2 Corinthians 9:8)?

8. Why does God make people rich (2 Corinthians 9:11)?

When talking about prosperity, the question is not, "Will God prosper me?" The question is, "What will I do with God's abundant provision?"

Application & Reflection

How has God blessed you with abundance? How can you use that abundance to bless others?

LESSON 3

PUTTING GOD FIRST

1. What did the Israelites do with the first portion of all God that provided for them (2 Chronicles 31:5–6)?

2. What part should we give to God (Proverbs 3:9)?

3. What happens as a result of giving the first part to God (Proverbs 3:10)?

4. Read Leviticus 27:30–32. Should we give a tithe of everything or of only our net pay? On the first part or the leftover part? Before or after taxes and other expenses?

5. Why did Malachi tell God's people they were under a curse (Malachi 3:9)?

6. How do people rob God (Malachi 3:8)?

7. How did God tell his people to test him (Malachi 3:10)?

8. What did God promise to do if his people would give him the whole tithe (Malachi 3:10–12)?

Application & Reflection

What did you learn from this lesson? How will you apply it to your life?

_____

_____

_____

_____

L E S S O N   4

EXTREME GENEROSITY

A story told in Luke 21:1-4 introduces the idea of extreme generosity—that is, sacrificial giving. Jesus is standing in the Jewish temple when a poor widow comes and gives two copper coins. It is not much, but apparently all she had. Jesus' reaction is instructive.

1. According to Jesus, who gave the most? Why (Luke 21:1-4)?

_____

_____

Read 2 Corinthians 8:1-5.

2. Paul bragged about the generosity of the Macedonian believers. How would you describe their situation (2 Corinthians 8:2)?

_____

_____

Here is the Macedonian formula for generosity:

severe trials + extreme poverty + overflowing joy = rich generosity

3. How much did the Macedonians give (2 Corinthians 8:3)?

_____

Some people spend all they can afford to spend—they're the ones who are always broke. Others spend less than they are able to spend—they're the ones who are constantly saving their money. Then there is that category of people who actually spend *more* than they have—they're the ones who are enslaved in debt.

On the flip side, some people give less than they are able to give. According to the Bible, they are *robbing* God. Others give what they are able. This is called *obedience*. Still others sacrificially give beyond their ability. These extreme givers, like the widow in the temple, are considered *heroes* of the faith.

4. Did Paul have to pressure the Macedonian believers to give? What was their attitude toward giving (2 Corinthians 8:4)?

_____

_____

Application & Reflection
What did you learn from this lesson and how will you apply it to your life?

_____

_____

_____

_____

What kind of giver are you?

- less than you can afford
- as much as you can afford
- more than you can afford

_____

_____

_____

_____

CHAPTER ELEVEN

EVANGELISM & WORLD MISSIONS

"All authority in heaven and on earth has been given to me. Therefore go and make disciples of all nations, baptizing them in the name of the Father and of the Son and of the Holy Spirit, and teaching them to obey everything I have commanded you. And surely I am with you always, to the very end of the age."

JESUS, MATTHEW 28:18-20

Before returning to heaven, Jesus promised to send his disciples the gift of the Holy Spirit. But he also gave his followers a job to do. The message of salvation was meant to be shared with everyone in every nation. Jesus wants us to proclaim this message—that is, to share the gospel—with our words ("teaching them . . .") and our deeds ("make disciples . . ."). The good news is that God himself has empowered us to be his representatives: "Surely I am with you always."

LESSON 1

EVERYONE IS A MINISTER

1. What "ministry" has God given to each believer (2 Corinthians 5:18)?

2. What "message" has God committed to us (2 Corinthians 5:19)?

3. What does *reconciliation* mean, and why do people need to be reconciled to God?

4. What is an "ambassador"?

5. What does it mean for us to be "Christ's ambassadors" (2 Corinthians 5:20)?

6. How will other people know that we are followers of Jesus (John 13:35)?

7. What was Paul's attitude toward sharing the gospel with non-Christians (Romans 1:14–16)?

verse 14

verse 15

verse 16

8. Paul, quoting the Old Testament prophet Joel, promises, "Everyone who calls on the name of the Lord will be saved" (Romans 10:13). But what must happen for people to call on the name of the Lord (verses 14–15)?

_____

9. God sent Peter to preach the gospel to a Roman centurion named Cornelius. Who did Cornelius gather to hear Peter speak (Acts 10:24)?

_____

10. What happened to those who heard Peter preach in Cornelius's house (Acts 10:44–48)?

_____

The story of Peter and Cornelius is amazing not just because of what happened when Peter preached, but also because of _who_ Peter's audience was. Cornelius was a Gentile—a non-Jew. In Peter's day, most Jews and Gentiles did not associate closely with each other. Even more startling, Cornelius was an officer in the Roman army that occupied the Jewish nation. In other words, Cornelius was Peter's natural enemy.

Jesus does not simply call us to share the gospel with our friends and loved ones. He goes further, teaching us to "love [our] enemies and pray for those who persecute [us]" (Matthew 5:44).

11. Where did Paul preach (Acts 20:20)?

_____

12. To whom did Paul preach (Acts 20:21)?

_____

13. What did Paul preach (Acts 20:21)?

_____

_____

Application & Reflection

What did you learn from this lesson? How will you apply it to your life? With whom—friends, loved ones, or even enemies—is God calling you to share the gospel?

_____

_____

_____

_____

_____

LESSON 2

BOLDNESS

For many believers in the first century (and many believers around the world today), preaching the gospel cost something—maybe a relationship with a friend or family member, maybe their livelihood. Many were imprisoned, physically abused, or even killed because they refused to be silent about their faith. In this lesson, we will explore how the early believers responded to such persecution.

1. Under the threat of persecution, what did the disciples pray for (Acts 4:29)?

   _____

   _____

2. What were the results of their prayer (Acts 4:31)?

   _____

   _____

3. According to Barnabas, how did Saul (Paul) preach—even in the face of a plot to kill him (Acts 9:22-28)?

   _____

   _____

EVANGELISM & WORLD MISSIONS

4. After Saul's conversion, how long did he wait until he preached the gospel (Acts 9:19–20)?

_____

5. What is the difference between a righteous man and a wicked man (Proverbs 28:1)?

_____

_____

6. What does Proverbs say about those who fear other people (Proverbs 29:25)?

_____

7. Paul requested prayers that he might preach the gospel in what manner (Ephesians 6:19–20)?

_____

Application & Reflection

What did you learn from this lesson? How will you apply it to your life? Take a moment to ask God to give you boldness to share the message of salvation with others.

_____

_____

_____

_____

_____

LESSON 3

SPIRITUAL CONFLICT AND EVANGELISM

1. What has happened to unbelievers (2 Corinthians 4:4)?

_____

_____

2. How are people taken captive (Colossians 2:8)?

3. What did Jesus come to do (Luke 4:18–21)?

4. Why did the Son of God appear (1 John 3:8)?

The Bible describes the church as the "body of Christ" (1 Corinthians 12:27). If we are Christ's body—his presence in the world today—then Jesus' mission is *our* mission. He has called us to proclaim good news to the poor, the captives, the blind, and the oppressed. He has called us to participate in destroying the devil's work. In other words, when we share the gospel with lost people, we are engaging in spiritual warfare. Jesus came to set captives free. He frees people as we speak the truth.

5. Who are we struggling against (Ephesians 6:12)?

6. What happened when Paul preached (Acts 16:14)?

7. What must happen if people are to come to Christ (John 6:44)?

Application & Reflection
What did you learn from this lesson? How will you apply it to your life?

LESSON 4

MIRACLES, SIGNS, AND WONDERS

1. When the disciples stepped out in faith and boldly preached the gospel, what happened (Acts 2:43; 3:16)?

2. Why did the people in Samaria pay close attention to Philip (Acts 8:6–8)?

Signs and wonders were not just for apostles. Philip was a faithful servant in the church whom God used to proclaim the gospel with miraculous power.

3. What were Paul and Barnabas doing when the lame man from Lystra was healed (Acts 14:5–10)?

Our part is to boldly preach God's salvation and pray for him to act. As we do this, God will work powerful miracles in people's lives. In other words, we do the preaching; he does the healing.

4. What did James instruct the church to do for those who were sick (James 5:14–15)?

5. What did Jesus promise to those with faith (John 14:12)?

6. How can we see "even greater things" (John 14:12–14)?

7. How was the crippled man at the Beautiful Gate healed (Acts 3:6–7, 16)?

8. How much authority is in the name of Jesus (Matthew 28:18)?

9. What happens at the mention of Jesus' name (Philippians 2:10–11)?

Acting in Jesus' name isn't like using a magic word. It's much better than that. To act in Jesus' name is to acknowledge his authority over everything. When we submit ourselves to his authority, he gives us the power to advance his kingdom.

10. What did Jesus say would happen if we have faith in him (Mark 11:23–24)?

11. What did Jesus say about the power of faith (Mark 9:23)?

12. What pleases God (Hebrews 11:6)?

Application & Reflection

How have you seen the power of God at work in your life? Think of a time when you boldly proclaimed the gospel. How did God act?

LESSON 5

TO THE ENDS OF THE EARTH

1. What did Jesus promise would happen when the Holy Spirit came on his followers (Acts 1:8)?

2. What is a *witness*?

3. What does it mean to be Christ's witness?

4. Where were Jesus' followers to be witnesses (Acts 1:8)?

5. What was the first promise Jesus gave to his followers (Matthew 4:19)?

6. What was the last command Jesus gave his disciples (Matthew 28:19)?

"Come" and "go" are the foundational commands of discipleship. Jesus calls us to "come" and follow him, becoming his disciples. But one key purpose of a disciple is to make more disciples—to "go."

7. What are we to do with the disciples we make (Matthew 28:19–20)?

_____

_____

8. What did Jesus promise to everyone who will "go and make disciples of all nations" (Matthew 28:19–20)?

_____

_____

9. What is the condition of the world in relation to the gospel?

Matthew 9:35–37 _____

John 4:35–36 _____

10. What did Jesus say we should pray for (Matthew 9:38)?

_____

11. Jesus died on the cross to purchase people from where (Revelation 5:9)?

_____

_____

Application & Reflection

What did you learn from this lesson? How will you apply it to your life? What part is God calling you to play in fulfilling his command to reach every nation with the gospel?

_____

_____

_____

CHAPTER TWELVE

RESURRECTION & JUDGMENT

The LORD reigns forever; he has established his throne for judgment. He rules the world in righteousness and judges the peoples with equity.

DAVID, PSALM 9:7-8

"God will bring into judgment both the righteous and the wicked, for there will be a time for every activity, a time to judge every deed."

THE TEACHER, ECCLESIASTES 3:17

Just as people are destined to die once, and after that to face judgment, so Christ was sacrificed once to take away the sins of many; and he will appear a second time, not to bear sin, but to bring salvation to those who are waiting for him.

HEBREWS 9:27-28

According to the Bible, all of us have three inescapable appointments: death, resurrection, and judgment. We all will die one day. We all will be raised again—but not just as disembodied spirits. And we all will be judged at the throne of God.

LESSON 1

DEATH AND RESURRECTION

1. What is everyone appointed to do once (Hebrews 9:27)?

2. Where will we all stand one day (Romans 14:10)?

3. Did Paul fear death? Why not (Philippians 1:21)?

Read 1 Corinthians 15. There are three popular views of death, but only one of them is based on God's Word.

Annihilationism is the view that human beings cease to exist at the moment of physical death. This view denies the eternal existence of the soul and the justice of God.

Reincarnation is the view that upon death, a person's soul passes into a new body of either the same or different species as punishment or reward. This view denies the biblical teaching of eternal judgment.

Resurrection is the biblical teaching the dead shall all rise, be judged, and be given either eternal punishment or eternal rewards.

4. What did Paul say to those who said there is no resurrection (1 Corinthians 15:13)?

_____

_____

5. What did Paul say is the result if Christ was not really resurrected (1 Corinthians 15:14–19)?

verse 14 _____

verse 15 _____

verse 16 _____

verse 17 _____

verse 18 _____

verse 19 _____

Paul insisted that because Christ has been raised from the dead, we will be raised from death as well.

6. What is the last enemy Christ will destroy (1 Corinthians 15:26)?

_____

7. How did Paul describe the resurrection body (1 Corinthians 15:42–44)?

verse 42 _____

verse 43 _____

verse 44 _____

8. Paul did not relate to Jesus as if he was still on the cross. How did Paul want to "know Christ" (Philippians 3:10)?

_____

_____

9. What did Paul hope to attain (Philippians 3:11)?

_____

_____

10. What was Paul's hope (Acts 24:15)?

_____

_____

11. How did Paul's belief in the resurrection affect the way he lived (Acts 24:16)?

_____

_____

12. Where is our citizenship (Philippians 3:20)?

_____

_____

13. What will our Savior do to our bodies (Philippians 3:21)?

_____

_____

14. To be alive "in the body" is to be what (2 Corinthians 5:6)?

_____

15. To be "away from the body" is to be what (2 Corinthians 5:8)?

_____

_____

16. Where must we all appear one day (2 Corinthians 5:10)?

_____

17. Why did Jesus share in our humanity (Hebrews 2:14)?

_____

_____

18. Who holds the power of death (Hebrews 2:14)?

_____

19. Who broke his power? How did he break it (Hebrews 2:14)?

_____

_____

20. How is it possible to be set free from the fear of death (Hebrews 2:15)?

_____

_____

Application & Reflection

What did you learn from this lesson? How will you apply it to your life?

_____

_____

_____

_____

LESSON 2

THE JUSTICE OF GOD AND THE SINFULNESS OF HUMANITY

Many of those who don't know God and assume that people are basically good wonder, "How can a loving God send people to hell?" But as we saw in chapter 1, the goodness of God's creation was scarred by humanity's sin. Once we see how sinful we are and how perfectly holy God is, we will wonder, "How can a holy God allow sinful people into heaven?"

1. What is the foundation of God's throne (Psalm 89:14)?

_____

2. What if we claim to be a Christian yet "walk in the darkness" (1 John 1:6)?

3. What if we claim to be without sin (1 John 1:8)?

4. What if we deliberately keep on sinning (Hebrews 10:26–27)?

5. What do you think it means to "trample the Son of God" and "insult the Spirit of grace" (Hebrews 10:28–29)?

6. Why is it a "dreadful thing" to fall into the hands of the living God (Hebrews 10:30–31)?

7. What are those with stubborn, unrepentant hearts doing (Romans 2:5)?

8. What can those who reject God's truth expect from him (Romans 2:8)?

9. What do those who believe in Jesus have? What about those who reject Jesus (John 3:36)?

10. How are those who believe in Jesus to speak and act (James 2:12)?

11. What if we live a "pretty good life" and "do our best" to follow God but disobey just once (James 2:10)?

12. What is the moral condition of every human (Romans 3:23)?

13. How can we be justified before God (Romans 3:24)?

14. What did the sacrificial death of Christ demonstrate (Romans 3:25–26)?

15. God is not only just, but also does what (Romans 3:26)?

Application & Reflection

What did you learn from this lesson? How will you apply it to your life?

LESSON 3

THE JUDGMENT OF SINNERS

1. What comes after death (Hebrews 9:27)?

2. Who will enter the kingdom of heaven (Matthew 7:21)?

3. What will Jesus say to those who called him Lord but did not really live under his lordship (Matthew 7:22–23)?

Read Matthew 25:31–46.

4. On judgment day, Jesus will separate the "sheep from the goats"–that is, the righteous from the wicked. What are the only two eternal destinations after judgment (Matthew 25:46)?

5. How is hell described in the following passages?

Matthew 13:41–42

Matthew 25:41

Mark 9:43

Luke 16:23–24

2 Thessalonians 1:9

6. Who will be judged in hell?

Matthew 23:29–33

Matthew 24:48–51

John 3:36

Romans 2:8

Revelation 20:15

Revelation 21:8

7. What do the following Scripture passages teach about the "fear of God"?

Deuteronomy 10:12

Ecclesiastes 12:13

Isaiah 8:13

Matthew 10:28

Luke 1:50

Acts 10:35

The Bible teaches that God is loving, kind, and compassionate. But he is also holy and just. That is why we are commanded to *fear* him— that is, to treat him with reverence and awe. We do not fear God because he is fickle or unreliable. Far from it! God will always show mercy to those who fear him (Luke 1:50).

Application & Reflection

What did you learn from this lesson? How will you apply it to your life? How do you "fear God" in your daily life?

LESSON 4

THE JUDGMENT OF SAINTS

All who repent of their sins and put faith in Christ will be with him in paradise forever. Because God is just and our justifier, we will not be judged with those who die apart from Christ. But our life work will be judged—not to determine our eternal destination, but to determine our eternal rewards.

1. What does Jesus do for us (1 Thessalonians 1:10)?

2. What did Paul tell the believers in Rome (Romans 14:10-12)?

3. What did Paul tell the believers in Corinth (2 Corinthians 5:10)?

Read 1 Corinthians 3:9–15.

4. What will the fire test on judgment day (1 Corinthians 3:13)?

5. What will we receive if our work survives God's judgment (1 Corinthians 3:14)?

6. What if our life's work is burned up in judgment (1 Corinthians 3:15)?

7. What did James say about the judgment of spiritual leaders (James 3:1)?

8. What did David say about the death of those who are faithful to the Lord (Psalm 116:15)?

9. What did John say about the death of a believer (Revelation 14:13)?

10. What must we believe about God (Hebrews 11:6)?

In 1 Corinthians 9:24–26, Paul compares the Christian life to an Olympic race, highlighting the need for endurance and discipline.

11. Athletes in ancient Rome competed for crowns made of perishable leaves and vines. What kind of crown does the Christian train for (1 Corinthians 9:25)?

12. What were Paul's thoughts about the possibility of making it to heaven (by the grace of God) only to be disqualified from receiving "the prize" (1 Corinthians 9:26–27)?

13. What was Paul's "crown" (Philippians 4:1)?

14. What was Paul's "hope," his "joy," his "crown" (1 Thessalonians 2:19)?

15. Who will be rewarded with the "crown of righteousness" (2 Timothy 4:7–8)?

16. Paul says the "crown of righteousness" is for those who long for Jesus' return. According to Peter, what should those who "look forward to the day of God" do (2 Peter 3:11–12)?

17. What reward does God give to those who persevere under severe trials (James 1:12)?

18. What must we do to receive the "victor's crown" (2 Timothy 2:4-5)?

19. What activities does God promise to reward?

Matthew 6:3–4

Matthew 6:6

Matthew 6:16–18

20. Revelation 4 describes four living creatures who circle the throne of God, worshiping him day and night. What do these heavenly beings do with their crowns (Revelation 4:9-10)?

21. Why is God worthy of our crowns (Revelation 4:11)?

Application & Reflection

What did you learn from this lesson? How will you apply it to your life?

EVERY NATION

Every Nation is a worldwide family of churches and ministries that exists to honor God by establishing Christ-centered, Spirit-empowered, socially responsible churches and campus ministries in every nation.

Since it was established in 1994, Every Nation has been making disciples, training leaders, and planting churches all over the world. Our vision is to see a multi-ethnic, multi-generational Church that will seek first the kingdom of God for the glory of Jesus Christ, about whom it is written: "With your blood you purchased for God persons from every tribe and language and people and nation" (Revelation 5:9).

For more information about Every Nation and its work around the world, please visit our websites and social media sites.

www.everynation.org

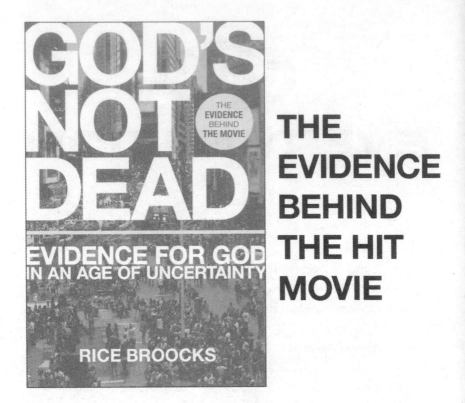

**THE
EVIDENCE
BEHIND
THE HIT
MOVIE**

THE GOAL OF *GOD'S NOT DEAD: EVIDENCE FOR GOD IN AN AGE OF Uncertainty* is straightforward: to help readers develop "a faith that is real and credible—and strong enough to help others find faith in God." With clear, easy-to-follow explanations of key concepts and controversies, *God's Not Dead* is apologetics for the twenty-first century, presented in layman's terms. Readers will be empowered not only to talk about their own faith with confidence but to lead others to a relationship with Jesus.

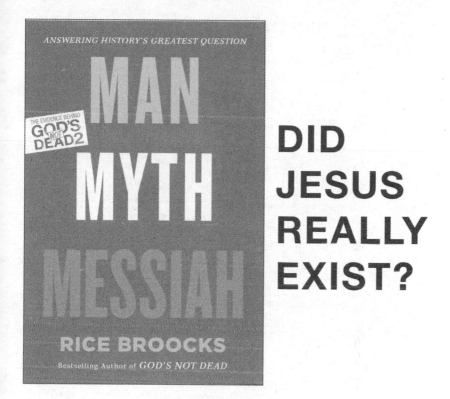

ANSWERING HISTORY'S GREATEST QUESTION

MAN
MYTH
MESSIAH

THE EVIDENCE BEHIND
GOD'S NOT DEAD 2

RICE BROOCKS

Bestselling Author of *GOD'S NOT DEAD*

DID
JESUS
REALLY
EXIST?

IN THIS FOLLOW-UP TO THE BOOK *GOD'S NOT DEAD* (THAT INSPIRED the movie), *Man, Myth, Messiah* looks at the evidence for the historical Jesus and exposes the notions of skeptics that Jesus was a contrived figure of ancient mythology. It also looks at the reliability of the Gospel records as well as the evidence for the resurrection that validates His identity as the promised Messiah.

W PUBLISHING GROUP

AN IMPRINT OF THOMAS NELSON

AVAILABLE WHEREVER BOOKS
AND DIGITAL BOOKS ARE SOLD.

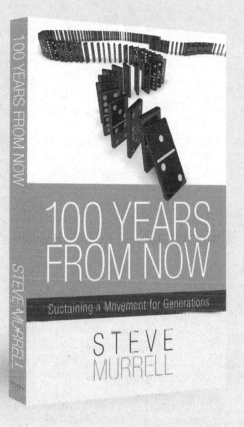
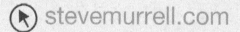

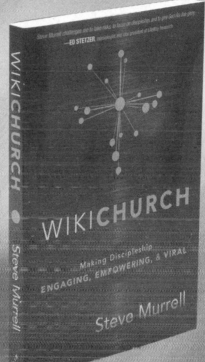